T0215037

Closing the Analytics Talent Gap

Data Analytics Applications
Series Editor: Jay Liebowitz

PUBLISHED

Data Analytics Applications in Education
by Jan Vanthienen and Kristoff De Witte
ISBN: 978-1-4987-6927-3

Data Analytics Applications in Latin America and Emerging Economies
by Eduardo Rodriguez
ISBN: 978-1-4987-6276-2

Data Analytics for Smart Cities
by Amir Alavi and William G. Buttlar
ISBN 978-1-138-30877-0

Data-Driven Law
Data Analytics and the New Legal Services
by Edward J. Walters
ISBN 978-1-4987-6665-4

Intuition, Trust, and Analytics
by Jay Liebowitz, Joanna Paliszkiewicz, and Jerzy Gołuchowski
ISBN: 978-1-138-71912-5

Research Analytics
Boosting University Productivity and Competitiveness through Scientometrics
by Francisco J. Cantú-Ortiz
ISBN: 978-1-4987-6126-0

Sport Business Analytics
Using Data to Increase Revenue and Improve Operational Efficiency
by C. Keith Harrison and Scott Bukstein
ISBN: 978-1-4987-8542-6

Data Analytics and AI
by Jay Liebowitz
ISBN: 978-0-3678-9561-7

Closing the Analytics Talent Gap

An Executive's Guide to Working with Universities

Jennifer Priestley and Robert McGrath

CRC Press
Taylor & Francis Group
Boca Raton   London   New York

CRC Press is an imprint of the
Taylor & Francis Group, an **informa** business

AN AUERBACH BOOK

First edition published 2021
by CRC Press
6000 Broken Sound Parkway NW, Suite 300, Boca Raton, FL 33487-2742

and by CRC Press
2 Park Square, Milton Park, Abingdon, Oxon, OX14 4RN

Library of Congress Cataloging-in-Publication Data
A catalog record for this book has been requested

ISBN: 978-0-367-75466-2 (hbk)
ISBN: 978-0-367-48690-7 (pbk)
ISBN: 978-1-003-04230-3 (ebk)

Typeset in Garamond
by KnowledgeWorks Global Ltd.

Contents

Preface

The seeds of this book began in 2016. We were both directors of academic graduate programs in analytics and data science. While we were in very different parts of the country – Durham, New Hampshire and Kennesaw, Georgia are 1,148 miles apart – and we were overseeing very different types of programs –a doctoral program and a master's program – we found that we were being asked the same questions from managers and executives of analytical organizations: *How can I recruit out of your program? I have a project – how do I reach out to your students? If we do research together who owns it? I have employees who need to "upskill" in analytics – can you help me with that? How much does all of this cost?*

As we engaged in discussions between the two of us, we learned that many of our academic colleagues at **Oklahoma State University, University of Alabama, University of Cincinnati, Wake Forest University**, were all engaged in similar conversations with organizations.

For many of us who oversee analytics programs, the opposite conversations were happening as well – *How can I bring a "real" analytical project in the classroom? How can I get "real" data to help my students develop the skills necessary to be a "data scientist? Is what I am teaching in the classroom aligned with the demands of the market for analytical talent?*

Historically, the academic domain and the corporate domain rarely intersected; as academics who worked in the private sector, we can tell you that the cultural chasms have been deep. But that gulf is narrowing. Today, there is an increasingly permeable membrane between academia and the private sector, with more collaboration and meaningful integration occurring between the two sectors than at any other time in history. Consider the following:

- Before 2006, there were no formal university programs in the country with the title "Data Science", or "Business Analytics". By 2020, largely in response to the demands of the private sector, there were over 300 programs at the master's level and almost 100 at the PhD level.
- Almost half of all individuals earning PhDs in computational disciplines enter the private sector after graduation.
- Multi-organization innovation and research labs, which include university faculty, graduate students, private sector R&D teams and public sector policy

contributors, are increasingly common; many of these labs publish more "academic" papers than traditional academic departments.

- In 2017, a quarter of all "academic" publications in data science journals included an author employed in the private sector with no academic affiliation.
- According to the U.S. Bureau of Labor Statistics, in 2019, the gap between the supply and demand of individuals with computational skills continues to grow, with estimates for the number of data scientists – and all iterations – surpassing 1 million open positions.
- In 2017, Amazon launched "AWS Machine Learning Research Awards", supporting research at universities (and non-profit institutions).
- In 2019, Google announced that they would be conferring PhD degrees.

At our own universities, we regularly see healthcare systems, financial service providers, manufacturing firms competing to hire the same student. At first glance, that makes no sense – after all, these are completely different industry domains. Just ten years ago, it was unheard of to see a big bank and a healthcare provider recruiting the same student. Today, its common place.

Organizations are facing previously unforeseen challenges related to the translation of massive amounts of data – structured and unstructured, static and in-motion, voice, text, image – into information to solve current challenges, and anticipate new ones. All while outpacing the competition and meeting increasingly complex demands of customers…frequently with employees whose skills have not kept pace with these tectonic data-centric shifts. So why would a bank and a healthcare provider want to hire the same student? Because while domain expertise is important, it is frequently subordinated; the bigger challenge is finding "data natives" who have the facility to work in a multi-faceted and complex data environment instead of finding a student with previous experience in banking.

Importantly, the advent of analytics and data science presents universities with unforeseen challenges. Unlike more traditional disciplines like mathematics or English, the organizational location of data science within a university is still not yet well defined – should it be housed in Computer Science? Statistics? Business? Or in an interdisciplinary center or institute? Data science curriculums are still nascent with little standardization and no accreditation. However, what is consistently recognized across the academic ecosystem is that data science – like Accounting, Medicine and Engineering – is really a discipline that is best learned through application. While most universities with data science programs have some requirement for experiential learning (e.g., applied projects, capstone courses, and internships), aligning these initiatives with companies can present challenges. Additionally, with the relatively new phenomena of individuals with PhDs pursuing careers in the private sector – while still engaging in meaningful and relevant research AND making more money than they would in academia – universities are experiencing their own "talent gap".

As those responsible for analytical teams consider strategies related to organizational data, strategic objectives and analytical talent, partnership with a university (or a portfolio of universities) can become a multi-faceted resource (or even a "secret weapon").

In our collective 50 years of academic experience (Bob is older), we have identified four broad objectives that companies – particularly those on the lower end of the analytics maturity continuum – have for partnering with universities in the context of analytics and data science:

■ New Hires and entry talent pipelines
■ Alternative Insights
■ Innovation and Research
■ Community Engagement

For a data science collaboration to be successful, both parties need to see benefits; organizational leaders need to also consider what the university will need to deem the collaboration successful. From our experiences as faculty and as academic administrators, universities have four broad objectives for partnering with companies in the context of analytics and data science:

■ Student Experiential Learning
■ Research
■ External Funding
■ Community Engagement

We wrote this book for managers of analytical organizations to help facilitate those conversations with universities and provide insights to some of those questions up front. We are also hoping that this book will broaden the aperture through which you think about universities – particularly in the context of analytics and data science.

In Chapter 1, we begin with an introduction to data science education. We address how data science has emerged (is emerging) as an academic discipline, how universities treat "data science" differently from "analytics", and why the academic location of a data science program within a university matters in the context of a corporate collaboration. In Chapter 2, we layout the roles and responsibilities of the people with whom you may come into contact at a university from faculty to deans, from career services to development (spoiler: they don't ALL want money). The chapter includes our "View from the Ground" where we have invited faculty, managers of analytical teams, and students to provide insights into how these partnerships "really" work. In this chapter, we include reflections from a senior data scientist with **The Home Depot** on the insights gained by serving on a university analytics advisory board. In Chapter 3, we address the unique opportunities and challenges of working with an undergraduate population, with specific emphasis on how to get the most out of analytical internships. We provide two case studies of undergraduate engagements – from the **University of New Hampshire** and from **North–West University in South Africa**. In Chapter 4, we focus on what you can expect from working with master's-level students. We include case studies of project courses with master's students from **Kennesaw State University** and from **Oklahoma State University**. We also highlight graduate collaboration from three perspectives: from a university analytics program director (**Georgia Tech**), from a corporate sponsor of a master's-level analytics project (**Shaw Industries**), and from a master's student (**University of New Hampshire**). Chapter 5 addresses the nuances of working with doctoral students and research faculty in data science, including the non-trivial issues of intellectual property assignment, scholarship, and publication. We include an interview with the leader of an innovation team from **Equifax** on the factors that contribute to a successful university research relationship. We also interview a doctoral student on their experiences working in a research lab supported with private sector funding. Finally, in Chapter 6, we address the role of continuing and professional education in analytics and data science, with specific examples from the **University of Dallas** and the collaboration between Uber and **Arizona State University**. We discuss the evolving role of the Certified Analytics Professional (CAP) credential as an emerging standardized credential and include a discussion with the Dean of a College of Continuing and Professional Education.

Acknowledgements

The authors would like to express their deep and sincere gratitude to all of those who contributed to the examples, experiences, and thoughtful reflections contained within these pages. We want to thank Chris Yasko, Cheryl Pressly, Khalifeh Al Jadda, and Erika Pullum for their invaluable insights as leaders of analytical teams. We want to recognize our academic colleagues Keith Werle, Goutam Chakraborty, Miriam McGaugh, Jeremiah Johnson, Karen Jin, Riaan de Jongh, Sherri Ni, and Tim Blumentritt for their candid case studies. We also want to thank Lauren Staples and Jordan Myerowitz for sharing their experiences as students working on corporate-sponsored analytical projects in their respective academic programs.

We would further like to acknowledge our students both present and past. Without their work, input, experiences, and lifelong connection to their professors and programs, this text would not have been possible. As academics, the authors have a deep connection with and appreciation for their past and present students who have plodded through analytic challenges and problems, toiled with models and methods, and surpassed all of our expectations when they reach those "ah ha" moments. You awe and inspire us. It is for you that we do what we do.

We owe a strong debt of gratitude to Chuck Larson who is the ever so skilled creator of all the cartoons found in the text. Your wit and skill with the pen define you sir. We would also like to thank everyone at CRC Press who worked to make this book a reality. From inception to editing to printing and all that comes after, you have all been a truly amazing team of professionals.

Last but never least, the authors personally wish to thank our families who supported our time glued to the computer and those close colleagues that put up with our harassing for content, edits or just thoughtful reflection. You know who you are.

About the Authors

Dr. Jennifer Priestley is a professor of Statistics and Data Science. Since 2004, she has served as the associate dean of the Graduate College and as the executive director of the Analytics and Data Science Institute at Kennesaw State University. In 2012, the SAS Institute recognized Dr. Priestley as the 2012 Distinguished Statistics Professor of the Year. She served as the 2012 and 2015 co-chair of the National Analytics Conference. Datanami recognized Dr. Priestley as one of the top 12 "Data Scientists to Watch in 2016".

She architected the first PhD Program in Data Science, which launched in February 2015.

Dr. Priestley has been a featured international speaker at The World Statistical Congress, The South African Statistical Association, SAS Global Forum, Big Data Week, Technology Association of Georgia, Data Science ATL, The Atlanta CEO Council, Predictive Analytics World, INFORMS, and dozens of academic and corporate conferences addressing issues related to the evolution of data science.

She has authored dozens of articles on Binary Classification, Risk Modeling, Sampling, Statistical Methodologies for Problem Solving, and Applications of Big Data Analytics.

Prior to receiving a PhD in Statistics, Dr. Priestley worked in the Financial Services industry for 11 years. Her positions included vice president of Business Development for VISA EU in London, as well as for MasterCard US and an analytical consultant with Accenture's strategic services group.

Dr. Priestley received a PhD from Georgia State University, an MBA from The Pennsylvania State University, and a BS from Georgia Institute of Technology.

**Dr. Robert McGrath** is the Everett B Sackett Professor of Health Management and Policy within the College of Health and Human Services at the University of New Hampshire. Since 2018 he has served as the chair of the Department of Health Management and Policy and the director of the Graduate Programs in Health Data Science. Prior to that time, he founded and directed the UNH Graduate Programs in Analytics and Data Science.

Dr. McGrath has been a program partner with the Northeast Big Data and Innovation Hub in the areas of data literacy and data ethics. He has been a featured national and international speaker at the Chengdu University and Chengdu Institute for Technology (China), the Northeast Big Data Conference, the Joint Statistical Association, SAS Global Forum, INFORMS, the American Association of Colleges of Nursing, the Association of University Programs in Health Administration, the American Public Health Association, the American College of Medical Genetics, and many other academic and corporate conferences addressing issues related to the evolution of data science and health analytics.

He is the author of two texts and numerous articles on analytics, data science, quantitative management methods, health policy evaluations and health outcomes.

Dr. McGrath received a PhD from Brandeis University, an MS from Harvard University, and a BS from the University of New Hampshire.

Chapter 1

Analytics and Data Science 101

From Plato to Davenport and Patil

A bulk of scientific discovery and learning throughout history has emerged largely from the work of universities. The origins of what we now call "universities" started with Plato's academy for philosophical thought – the first "university", where great notions were deliberated en masse. However, as scientific study began in earnest, those next-generation critical thinkers, from Rene Descartes to Newton to DaVinci, realized the need for structure for any empirical meaningfulness to be attained. This need gave rise to the formal disciplines and what today we call the "Academy". Disciplines such as Mathematics, Physics, Chemistry, and the Arts, thrived in dedicated settings for discovery, modes for inquiry, models for explanation, and avenues for dissemination of findings.

With science came improvements in measurement (microscope and telescope) and practice (surgery and engineering), prompting academic fields to become deeper and evermore specialized. For much of the past hundred years, scientific advancement has been characterized by continued specialization due to improved measurement, the need to propagate the careers of academics, and the need of the academy to support its own claim to the gold star of knowledge, which has come to define the current landscape of universities worldwide. In other words ... academics and academic disciplines have historically thrived in highly siloed environments with little to no engagement outside their field.

> As two people with a combined 50 years of experience in academic settings, we can tell you that no organization does "siloes" better than university.

Only recently have previously siloed academic environments begun to create receptive points of intersection. Consider relatively new fields of study such as biochemistry, behavioral economics, and biomedical engineering – which have evolved through the willingness and intellectual entrepreneurism of researchers and practitioners who saw the value of collaborating outside of their siloed discipline. Similarly, the field of data science has emerged from outside of traditional academic siloes through the intersection of the established disciplines of statistics and computer science.

The term "data science" is actually not new. Its first references can be traced back to computer scientist Peter Naur in 1960 and from statistician John W. Tukey in 1962. Tukey wrote:

> *For a long time I thought I was a statistician, interested in inferences from the particular to the general. But as I have watched mathematical statistics evolve, I have … come to feel that my central interest is in data analysis.*

> **(Tukey, 1962)**

A reference to the term "data science" as an academic discipline within statistics was made in the proceedings of the Fifth Conference of the International Federation of Classification Societies in 1996[1]. In 1997, during his inaugural lecture as the H. C. Carver Chair in Statistics at the University of Michigan, Jeff Wu called for statistics to be renamed "data science" and statisticians to be renamed "data scientists"[2].

> While many in the field of statistics have a justifiable claim on being part of the "founding members club" of data science, statistics – and statisticians – were not prepared for the evolution of data.

Consider Figure 1.1. In the field of statistics, most formal instruction – if it goes beyond the theory – involves the translation of data into information that would be characterized as "Small, Structured, and Static" (think Excel spreadsheets) using traditional methods and supervised modeling techniques. However, as data evolves beyond the structured files into images, text, and streaming data, into the

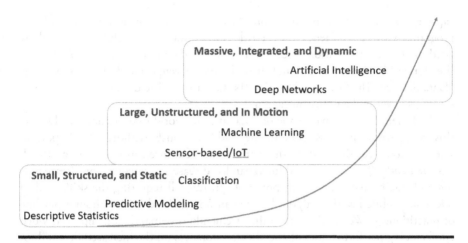

Figure 1.1   Evolution of data.

second and third boxes of Figure 1.1, practitioners (and students) need integrated concepts from computer science – and increasingly from engineering and from the humanities – as well as context from the domain where the data originated. Statistics is needed ... but not sufficient. Computer science is needed ... but not sufficient. Marketing ... finance ... engineering ... ethics ... all needed ... but not sufficient.

An examination of the popularity of the term "Data Science" from Google Trends, indicates that the term was a subject of the search engine in the early days of 2004. See Figure 1.2. Around the end of 2012, we see an inflection point, with "Data Science" experiencing a surge as a popular search term. While there are multiple points of explanation for the timing of this inflection – our increased

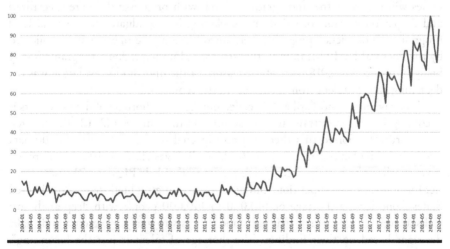

Figure 1.2   Google Trends index for "Data Science" (2004–2020).

capacity to access, capture, and store data to the growing number of academic programs with "data science" in the title – there was one article that is regularly cited as starting the national conversation about data science. In October 2012, the Harvard Business Review published Thomas Davenport and D. J. Patil's article "Data Science: The Sexiest Job of the 21st Century"[3]. The dating profiles for data scientists never looked the same again.

And then came the pandemic of 2020 and the world forever changed. During this long period, most everyone in the world cautiously withdrew for important safety reasons, yet the work of the world continued, often in new ways and with new demands. We saw the need for expanded disease surveillance, for disease testing and tracing data and for mapping of spread – all requiring the skills of data scientists. Public health analytics became an unparalleled field without a pipeline of practitioners. We continue to realize tremendous demands for improved video conferencing platforms, for enhanced video storage, and the increased demand for online entertainment content, all of which create mineable data. Our increased global reliance on home delivery and distribution services like Amazon, UPS, and Federal Express will have profound impacts on our notions of supply chain efficiencies. And all of this increases the need for data security, privacy, and exacerbate the wealth of ethical considerations that have emerged along the way.

Universities Answer the Call

While the first university programs in "Data Science" – including "Analytics" – emerged in 2006–2007, the evolution of the discipline has been, well … "lumpy". As we will discuss in more detail in Chapter 4, the first wave of data science programs emerged at the master's level. This is unusual; typically, academic disciplines will evolve at the undergraduate level, with progressively more specialized and deeper outlets for formal study developing into graduate and doctoral level programs. Data science programs were introduced at the master's level, followed by the doctoral level (2015), with the first formal undergraduate programs finally being introduced in 2018. Part of the reason for the unorthodox evolution was the deafening call for talent from all sectors of the economy.

The Davenport and Patil article called out "… The shortage of data scientists is becoming a serious constraint in some sectors". In the same year (2012), the research firm Gartner[4] reported that there was an expected shortage of over 100,000 data scientists in the United States by 2020 (the reality was closer to 10x this number). A year earlier, the heavily cited McKinsey Report[5] titled "Big data: The next frontier for innovation, competition, and productivity" highlighted that …"the United States alone faces a shortage of 140,000 to 190,000 people with deep analytical skills as well as 1.5 million managers and analysts to analyze big data and make decisions based on their findings. The shortage of talent is just the beginning". In 2014, the consulting firm Accenture reported that more than 90 percent of its clients planned to hire people with data science expertise, but more than 40 percent cited a lack of talent as the number one problem[6].

Universities, not typically known for their responsiveness, ramped up programs at lightning speed (by academic standards).

However, if you wanted to recruit for "data science" talent at a university, where would you go? Should you go to the College of Computing? Would it be in the College of Business? Is it in the Department of Mathematics? Statistics? Is there even a Department of Data Science?

If you are not sure where you would go, that would make you incredibly normal – and one of the reasons we wrote this book. There is more variation in the housing of data science than any other academic discipline on a university campus. Why the variation? And why should you care?

The answer to the first question – Why the variation? – may not be straight-forward. The Prussian statesman Otto Von Bismarck[7] is quoted as saying, "If you like laws and sausages, you should never watch either one being made". As in any organization, not all academic programs are a function of long-term, well-considered strategic planning – many programs evolve at the intersection of resources, needs, and opportunity. As universities began to formally introduce data science programs around 2006, there was little consistency regarding where this new discipline should be housed. Given the "academic ancestry" of statistics and computer science, as well as the domain specific areas of application (e.g., healthcare, finance, marketing, manufacturing) – it is not surprising that there is variation of placement of programs across the academic landscape. See Figure 1.3.

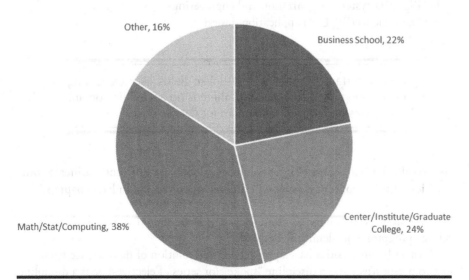

Figure 1.3 Academic location of programs in "data science", "analytics", and "machine learning"[8].

Exacerbating this, we do not yet have a universal consensus as to what set of competencies should be common to a data science curriculum – again largely due to its transdisciplinary foundations. The fields of computer science, mathematics, statistics, and almost every applied field (business, healthcare, engineering) have professional organizations and long-standing models for what constitutes competency in those fields. Simply combining them in an additive nature would make any such curriculum unyielding, ineffective, and not reflective of a unified discipline – or the demands of the marketplace. Importantly, these disciplines have different vocabularies, and describe similar concepts using different terms.

The most comprehensive approach to a standardized data science curriculum has been conducted by an open source effort, called the "Edison Data Science Framework"[9]. A list of topics for inclusion in data science programs is provided below:

1. Statistical methods and data analysis
2. Machine learning
3. Data mining
4. Text data mining
5. Predictive analytics
6. Modeling, simulation, and optimization
7. Big Data infrastructure and technologies
8. Infrastructure and platforms for data science
9. Cloud computing
10. Data and applications security
11. Big Data systems organization and engineering
12. Data science/Big Data application design

> It is important to reiterate that unlike fields like accounting, engineering, medicine, and law, there is no accrediting organization or standardized curriculum for data science.

As a result, the "data science" curriculum may look very different at different universities. This is a concept that we will discuss in more detail in later chapters.

The second question might be more relevant – Why should you care where a data science program is academically housed?

Generally, universities have approached the evolution of data science from one of two perspectives – as a discipline "spoke" (or series of electives) or as a discipline "hub" (as a major). See Figure 1.4.

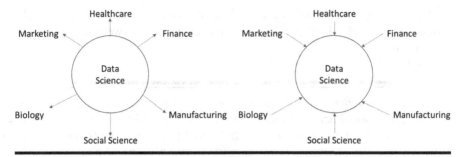

Figure 1.4 Data science and analytics programs as academic "Hubs" and "Spokes".

Programs that are "hubs" – reflecting the model on the left – have likely been established as a "major" field of study. These programs are likely to be housed in a more computational college (e.g., Computing, Science, Statistics) or research unit (like a Center or an Institute) and will focus on the "science of the data". They tend to be less focused on the nuances of any individual area of application. Hub programs will (generally) allow (encourage) their students to take a series of electives in some application domain (i.e., students coming out of a hub program may go into Fintech, but they may also go into healthcare – their major is "data"). Alternatively, programs that are "spokes" – reflecting the model on the right – are more likely to be called "analytics" and are more frequently housed in colleges of business, medicine, and the humanities. Programs that are "spokes" are (generally) less focused on the computational requirements and are more aligned with applied domain-specific analytics. Students coming out of these programs will have stronger domain expertise and will better understand how to integrate results into the original business problem but may lack deep computational skills. Students coming out of "hub" programs will likely be more comfortable moving along the continuum of data types highlighted in Figure 1.1, with students coming out of "spoke" programs, to be more likely work with data that is "Small, Structured, and Static" (which is actually sufficient for many organizations). Neither is "wrong" or "better" – the philosophical approaches are different. In addition, programs are constrained by the number of "credit hours"/courses that can be included. Most undergraduate programs will have about 40 courses in total – with less than 20 allocated to their "major". Most master's programs will have closer to 10 courses, while PhD programs are four to six years in duration but are heavily focused on research. As a result of these programmatic constraints, program directors have had to prioritize some concepts over others. Programs at each of these levels will be covered in Chapters 3, 4, and 5, respectively.

An ongoing longitudinal study tracking the salaries and educational backgrounds of data scientists[10] provides a similar distinction between data scientists and analysts:

> *... predictive analytics professionals ... (are) those who can apply sophisticated quantitative skills to data describing transactions, interactions, or other behaviors to derive insights and prescribe actions ... Data scientists ... are a subset of predictive analytics professionals who have the computer science skills necessary to acquire and clean or transform unstructured or continuously streaming data, regardless of its format, size, or source.*

In other words, all data science includes "analytics", but all analytics does not include "data science". Referring to the list of topics from the Edison Framework above, "analytics" programs would be more aligned with topics 1–5, where "data science" programs would be more likely to cover the full list. Throughout this book, we will refer to academic programs as "data science", with specific distinctions for "analytics" programs as needed.

A Wide Range of Solutions

Over the next five chapters, we will detail how managers of analytical organizations can leverage university collaborations to address the unprecedented challenges and opportunities that have emerged through the evolution of data and the rise of data science. Examples include:

■ The need to develop a reliable pipeline of "known" and consistent talent – at the undergraduate, master's, and doctoral levels. And the opportunity to contribute to updates and edits to the curriculum producing that talent as appropriate.
■ Working with faculty and doctoral students to facilitate innovation, research, and development for new products and services. Many companies use research collaboration as a way to position their organization as a "thought leader" in their industry.
■ Access to faculty to provide "ad hoc" employee workshops and training.
■ Formal opportunities for existing employees to "upskill" their knowledge.
■ Partnering with universities to contribute to the local community for "data science for social good".

As we will discuss in the next chapter, at their core, universities do two things: they teach and they discover new knowledge. In the context of data science, while many universities do both well, they will have different approaches, different points of emphasis, and will have different motivations for working with you.

Endnotes

1. https://cds.cern.ch/record/2027752?ln=en Accessed August 2, 2020.
2. https://en.wikipedia.org/wiki/C_F_Jeff_Wu Accessed August 3, 2020.
3. https://hbr.org/2012/10/data-scientist-the-sexiest-job-of-the-21st-century Accessed August 2, 2020.
4. https://blogs.gartner.com/doug-laney/defining-and-differentiating-the-role-of-the-data-scientist/ Accessed August 3, 2020.
5. https://www.mckinsey.com/business-functions/mckinsey-digital/our-insights/big-data-the-next-frontier-for-innovation Accessed August 2, 2020.
6. https://www.accenture.com/us-en/_acnmedia/Accenture/Conversion-Assets/DotCom/Documents/Global/PDF/Industries_14/Accenture-Big-Data-POV.pdf Accessed August 3, 2020.
7. https://en.wikipedia.org/wiki/Otto_von_Bismarck Accessed August 4, 2020.
8. This data was aggregated by the authors from public academic websites.
9. https://edison-project.eu/sites/edison-project.eu/files/attached_files/node-447/edison-mc-ds-release2-v03.pdf Accessed August 2, 2020.
10. https://www.burtchworks.com/big-data-analyst-salary/big-data-career-tips/the-burtch-works-study/ Accessed August 2, 2020.

Chapter 2

Navigating Universities – Where to Start

Universities 101

Most of us are familiar with universities in some way. You likely attended one or perhaps more than one. You likely have also had the notion that a university could be helpful in filling your organizational needs for talent. If your organization is large enough, you may have Human Resource representatives or even talent specialists that visit job fairs, university recruiting days, engineering or programming hackathons, and business competitions. Your organization may have a portfolio of universities they target for hiring. But what you may not have fully considered are the other reasons and opportunities for partnering with universities well beyond hiring – specifically those around research, innovation, consulting, community engagement, and current employee training and continuing education. Universities' historic core functions are to discover new knowledge, to train, and to educate. Some universities offer a more specialized curriculum while some provide a more generalized liberal arts curriculum (think Cal Tech vs. Wellesley College). But before we discuss this universe of differences and ultimately how to work with analytics and data science programs – which also have differences – some generalizations are necessary.

Most people are not at all familiar with how the work of universities gets done. In fact, the very term "university" connotes a very different scope of work than does "college", or "institute". There are other classifications within the university structure that depend on the number and types of programs that are offered, the number of doctoral degrees conferred annually, the amount of research conducted by faculty, the size of the institution, and a host of other factors.

> You should consider different (multiple) types of universities for collaboration for different organizational objectives – no university can be all things to all organizations.

Consider an automotive example – if your work requires hauling bricks, a ¾ ton pickup truck might fit the bill. If your goal is to commute an hour a day as cheaply as possible, an electric vehicle might be the best fit. A sports car with a manual transmission might be fun to drive (and sadly a dying art), but a sedan with an automatic transmission might be a more practical (albeit less fun) alternative to accomplish the same basic transportation objectives. Like the array of options for vehicles, so too do universities provide options for engagement in analytics and data science, and like cars, they all come with different base options and upgrade potentials. And at the risk of extending the automotive analogy too far, the highest end of a luxury automobile brand may have the top rating from a publication like *Consumer Reports*, but that does not mean that a less expensive model from the same automaker will perform as reliably. Similarly, universities at the top of the rankings earn those rankings largely because of their external research funding (most coming from the federal government) and academic publications, which has very little to do with the typical undergraduate experience or the faculty's ability (or interest) to engage with the private sector. More on that later.

Beyond the walls of the university, faculty come in different flavors. Some professors exclusively teach and have no research responsibilities, while some exclusively do research and have little or no interaction with students. One of the authors recently had a conversation with a research faculty colleague at a large university that generates over $1 billion (with a "b") a year in external research funding (primarily from the U.S. Department of Defense). The university in question has almost 30,000 students. The faculty member said, "*I hear that we have students, but I have never actually seen one on campus*". Needless to say, that faculty does not spend much time in the classroom. Or go to football games.

All of this is to suggest that the professor you email to start a collaboration in analytics and data science, has a specific set of incentives at work that may *promote* your organization's intended engagement or *prevent* it. You may have attempted to work with a faculty member in the past who was less than accommodating – our colleague who never met a student has zero incentive to take your call or collaborate with you (he has no incentive to take our call). Perhaps you would like to explore teaching a course or guest lecture in a course as a starting point to engage students, but found it difficult to gain any traction with faculty.

The flip side of this, of course, are conversations most academics have had with corporate executives where the assumption is that after a full career, they want to semi-retire at the local university, imparting wisdom to young eager students. I often hear the common retort at dinner parties after learning of my profession:

"After I retire I am going to teach at a university". (Aside, this is not the best way to gain professor friends.)

However, with some background information and context related to incentives and expectations for faculty and administrators across all of the different sizes and types of universities, there are rich opportunities to make integration between your company and a university partner mutually successful – and importantly can provide benefit to the students. We will discuss these perspectives in the coming sections.

Illustrations have been created especially for this book by Charles Larson.

What Do Universities Actually Do?

For all of the text that you will find in a university's mission statement, universities do two primary things: they teach and develop new knowledge. They also house many students and so need to have the necessary physical and virtual breadth of infrastructure to accomplish that. And of course, they play sports (some better than others). However, unless your collaboration hinges on recruiting for the New England Patriots, it is likely the products of the first two that have led you to seek out a partnership. Universities are divided into many sub-units, much as a company may be and these too can influence the desire on the part of the university to engage in some activities over others. Universities often have schools or colleges (e.g., the Business School, College of Engineering) that are further divided into departments where faculty typically have an "academic home" (e.g., the Department of Finance, the Department of Industrial and Systems Engineering).

Many universities have interdisciplinary research entities that span departments or even colleges where faculty share time or can have joint appointments for research activities. Interdisciplinary centers and institutes are particularly fertile environments for multi-party research initiatives that involve the public, private, and academic sectors. The National Science Foundation facilitates these types of initiatives through their IUCRC (Industry-University Cooperative Research Centers) grants[1]. These interdisciplinary research centers will be addressed in more detail in Chapter 5, in the context of working with data science doctoral students in data science.

We will discuss teaching and faculty designations later in this chapter, but first we examine academic institutions as a whole.

University Classifications and the Role of Research

Institutions of higher education are classified according to the Carnegie Classification of Institutions of Higher Education[2]. The classifications examine both graduate and undergraduate instructions, including type of programs (STEM-focused, liberal arts focused), length (primarily 2-year, 4-year), and size (small, medium, and large) among other classifiers. See Table 2.1.

As an example, Table 2.2 shows a Carnegie Classification report for two institutions: The University of Michigan in Ann-Arbor and Centre College in Danville, KY.

What does this mean and why should you care when partnering with this institution? First, the University of Michigan is classified as "Doctoral Universities:

Table 2.1   U.S. Universities and Colleges by Classification (2018)[2]

Classification	Number	Percentage
Doctoral University: Very High Research Activity	131	3.03%
Doctoral University: High Research Activity	135	3.12%
Doctoral University: Professional	152	3.52%
Master's Colleges and Universities	685	15.84%
Baccalaureate Colleges	575	13.30%
Baccalaureate/Associate's Colleges	262	6.06%
Associate's Colleges	1,000	23.13%
Other	1,384	32.01%
Grand Total	**4,324**	**100.00%**

Table 2.2 Carnegie Classification Report: University of Michigan, and Centre College[2]

Carnegie Attribute	University of Michigan, Ann-Arbor, MI	Centre College, Danville, KY
Level	4-year or above	4-year or above
Control	Public	Private
Student Population (Fall 2017)	46,002	1,450
Classification	Doctoral University: Very High Research Activity	Undergraduate College with Arts and Science focus
Size and Setting	4-year, large, primarily residential	4-year, small, highly residential
External Research Funding (2018)	$1,530,139,000	$0 reported

Very High Research Activity", meaning they have a high proportion of research faculty and have many active research initiatives going on across a wide range of disciplines, including medicine. Note their external research funding - $1.5 billion. Again with a "b". In fact, the University of Michigan is ranked as the second largest university in external research funding in the United States behind Johns Hopkins University. Almost all faculty at the University of Michigan are going to be evaluated heavily on their research productivity – with emphasis on the amount of externally funded research grants they oversee. To be sure, it is likely difficult to be hired into a faculty position at the University of Michigan without evidence of grant funding and a strong publication record. This information would be important if your interests were in developing new knowledge or perhaps finding a partner with cutting edge research facilities and a large infrastructure to support research labs. However, it would also behoove you to inquire about the extent to which faculty and graduate students' availability outside of their research requirements or restrictions on their time or instrumentation, for example. Also, because data science is inherently interdisciplinary, how those units share faculty and students, and the extent to which they integrate their research, would be important for a potential external collaborator to understand.

Alternatively, Centre College – listed as a "College That Changes Lives[3]" – has limited emphasis on research and has an exclusively undergraduate mission. The faculty all teach and have limited expectation for research or pressure to generate research-related funding. A college like Centre might be a strong collaborative partner if your needs are explicitly aligned with recruiting entry level talent. It is also a reminder that there are over 4,000 institutions of higher learning in the United

States and organizations should consider partnering with institutions beyond those consistently at the top of the rankings.

The second point related to Table 2.1 is that institutions like the University of Michigan have very wide ranges of degrees and areas of study. This would be important, if for example, you were interested in engaging in a research initiative that might cross multiple departments. Consider an innovation that involves the development of new sensors related to customer movements in a retail store. You would need faculty who were well versed in electrical engineering, but also in marketing, operations research, and data science. Working within an interdisciplinary framework at an institution like the University of Michigan might take some time to navigate, where navigating within a smaller college like Centre is less complex, but may or may not have the specific program of study that you need to fill your positions or support your research objectives. To that end, it is important to know *why* you are approaching *this specific* institution – what is it that they do well that has attracted you to them? To assist with this, we have created a non-exhaustive checklist of things to consider at the end of this chapter to have ready before approaching your higher education partner.

Teaching and Training

Universities offer degrees, and more increasingly also offer opportunities for continuing education, corporate training, digital badges, and micro-certifications (see Chapter 6). People seek out universities largely because they are accredited by various bodies that ensure the content is appropriate and that the faculty have the appropriate credentials to certify the educational knowledge competently. Degrees come in a variety of forms – associate degrees, bachelor's degrees of either science or arts, graduate certificates, master's degrees, and doctoral degrees which may be doctorates of philosophy or professional/clinical doctorates. Each of these also has a different set of requirements and many are accredited by formal boards. A Master of Business Administration (MBA), for example, must be granted by a business school accredited by the Association to Advance Collegiate Schools of Business (AACSB)[4], while engineering programs are accredited by the Accreditation Board for Engineering and Technology (ABET)[5]. While there is no accrediting body for analytics and data science, there is an emerging Certified Analytics Professional (CAP) credential that is discussed in more detail in Chapter 6. We discuss the details of formal analytics and data science degrees at the undergraduate, master's, and doctoral levels in Chapters 3, 4, and 5, respectively.

As you approach a university for collaboration – whether at the undergraduate, master's, or doctoral level – you will have to deal with faculty. In the next section, we try to provide some insight into working with faculty and why they may or may not return your call.

Incentives – Why Would a Faculty Member Take Your Call?

Being a faculty person is a job. We say this because there is a lingering rumor that being a faculty person consists of wandering the woods thinking about lofty ideas, returning to one's library for some further contemplative thought, a pipe and a tea, and the occasional visit to the classroom where students are quickly dismissed in theater style – or so classic films would have you believe. The reality on the ground is not that. In fact, neither one of us even owns a pipe.

Faculty, like all employees, have performance expectations. At our university, we utilize an "eighths system" for faculty performance agreements, whereby all full-time faculty divide their work into eight units. These units are typically divided among teaching, research, and service in some combination, or administrative work and other duties such as advising students. Faculty can have a wide variation in their split among these areas, which can impact their available time. Not all faculty must address each of these areas – such as our colleague mentioned above who is exclusively dedicated to research and has never actually seen a student. Understanding expectations for how faculty are incented will help when considering with whom and how to start a conversation related to collaborating and engagement. Table 2.3 is an example of expectations for faculty workload from Drexel University.

Three things are important here. The first point is that Drexel University is classified as "Doctoral University: Very High Research Activity" just like the University of Michigan. Most universities in this category will have a similar set of faculty expectations, again with some faculty having exclusively research (non-teaching) responsibilities. The second point is that most faculty have some combination of research, teaching, and service responsibilities – faculty will be considering an opportunity to work with you through one (or more) of these lenses. An important consideration for your project is that many collaborations can fit into several of these requirements simultaneously and thus can help support the level of assessed impact the faculty member is making, which in turn makes the endeavor more attractive – meaning that they are more likely to take your call. In other words, if you are trying to work with a faculty member, which of these areas – teaching, service, or research – will your project fall into?

The Taxonomy of Faculty

Tenured Faculty

No doubt you have heard of "tenure". Basically, tenure is a commitment on behalf of the university to the faculty member that they can publish and teach there for the rest of their career. It protects a faculty member's "academic freedom" to research or

Table 2.3   Example Policy Statement on Faculty Workload, Drexel University[6]

INSTRUCTION

Faculty whose work assignments include instruction must demonstrate teaching excellence that draws upon the instructor's depth and breadth of scholarship. Following are examples of workload functions addressing instruction.

- Regular teaching assignment
- Preparation of innovative teaching materials or instructional techniques or design and development of new curricula
- Development of innovative courses
- Course coordination involving mentoring/teaching of other course instructors
- Contribution to a department's/program's instructional program
- Direction of individual student work, e.g., independent studies, theses or dissertations, special student projects, and informal student seminars
- Administration of teaching, e.g., multiple sections, team taught
- Academic advisement which is integrally related to the learning process and to course outcomes
- Publication of textbooks or articles that reflect the faculty member's teaching contributions and scholarship
- Presentation of papers on teaching before learned societies
- Selection for special teaching activities outside of the University, especially outside the United States, e.g., Fulbright awards, special lectureships, panel presentations, seminar participations, and international study and development projects
- Membership on special bodies concerned with teaching, e.g., accreditation teams and special commissions
- Receipt of competitive grants/contracts to fund innovative teaching activities or to fund stipends for students
- Membership on panels to judge proposals for teaching grants/contracts
- Invitation to testify before governmental groups concerned with educational programs
- Supervision of students being trained in clinical activities in practical and/or field sites

RESEARCH OR OTHER CREATIVE SCHOLARLY ACTIVITIES

Faculty whose work assignments include research or other creative scholarly activities should clearly demonstrate excellence in these endeavors.

Following are examples of workload functions addressing research or other creative scholarly activities.

- Publication of articles, books, monographs, bulletins, reviews, and other scholarly works by reputable journals, scholarly presses, and publishing houses that accept works based on rigorous review and approval by peers in the discipline
- Receipt of competitive grants and/or contracts to finance the development of ideas
- Refereed presentations (e.g., professional conferences)
- Supervision of publishable undergraduate research project(s),
- Supervision of graduate research
- Patents
- Consulting
- Juried exhibitions of art works
- Appointment as consultant to state, national, and/or international public and private groups engaged in scholarly and/or artistic endeavor
- Development of processes or instruments useful in solving problems relevant to the mission and needs of the faculty members unit
- Selection for tour of duty at special institutes for advanced study
- Presenting testimony before governmental groups concerned with research or other creative scholarly activities

SERVICE

These service listings are necessarily lengthy to accommodate the diverse activity that may be typical of a particular unit. The service workload functions are to be used for workload reporting and are intended to complement tenure and promotion criteria but not to extend or substitute for them. Refer to the tenure and promotion policy for tenure and promotion documentation. The lengthy number of the service functions should not be construed as having more weight than the instruction or research functions.

PUBLIC SERVICE

Public service is the application of knowledge through research, teaching, and technical assistance to the solution of societal problems. Faculty whose work assignments are in public service must devise creative ways to serve the public. Following are examples of workload functions addressing public service.

- Providing information, advice, or assistance to governmental bodies, i.e., congress, State Legislature, City Council, committees or commissions of government, etc., or providing testimony at hearings of governmental bodies

■ Provide educational needs assessment, program development, training, consultation, and technical assistance to local, state, national, and/or international organizations

■ Identify, develop, and render service to individuals, communities, organizations, and public agencies in support of their own purposes and functions

■ Furnish leaders and groups with objective research results and other resource information for decision-making

■ Design and conduct feasibility studies, field-test basic knowledge, develop procedural and technical manuals, and provide group instruction on and off campus

■ Development and application of effective ways to identify problems and assess needs in a service area

■ Mentor people nationally and internationally to study the faculty member's work and innovations

■ Disseminate in the appropriate media the faculty member's service work and innovations

■ Development of instruments and/or processes useful in solving persistent problems in a service area

■ Serve on special bodies concerned with service

■ Receipt of grants and/or contracts to finance development and delivery of service innovations

■ Serving on panels judging grant/contract proposals for service innovations

Service – University Governance. University governance includes activities required to study University needs, to decide procedures for meeting those needs, and to implement those decisions. Faculty members are responsible for contributing to the myriad processes that move the University forward to carrying out its mission. Following are examples of workload functions addressing service as University Governance.

■ Serve in membership and/or leadership roles in University level activities, e.g., the faculty senate, special ad hoc and standing committees, etc.

■ Serve in membership and/or leadership roles in college/school level activities, e.g., special ad hoc and standing committees, etc.

■ Serve in membership and/or leadership roles in departmental/program level activities, e.g., special ad hoc and standing committees, etc.

■ Consistently displays collegiality and good departmental citizenship, including recruiting activities

- Carry out administrative responsibilities at the appropriate level(s)
- Serve in special assignments such as representing the University at national and/or international meetings
- Publish books, articles, and give speeches pertaining to governance in higher education; these works being rigorously reviewed and accepted by peers

Service – Other Professional Activities. Other professional activities include work within professional associations and learned societies and assistance to one's colleagues. Following are examples of workload functions addressing service as Other Professional Activities.

- Election to offices in professional associations and learned societies
- Serve on important state, national, and/or international committees in professional organizations
- Serve as editor or associate editor for professional journal
- Serve as consultant on problems appropriate to the disciplines
- Membership on editorial boards reviewing publications, panels judging grant/contract proposals, juries judging artworks

---

publish topics that may be unpopular. Tenured faculty are typically at the rank of "Full Professor" or "Associate Professor" (see Table 2.4) and would have progressed through the "tenure-track" process.

Fully tenured faculty have different incentives and expectations than do faculty on the "tenure-track" (see below). While there is still an expectation for publication, they do not need the same level of productivity. Tenured faculty are still reviewed regularly. This "post tenure" review is required to show that the faculty has become an expert contributor to their field and has assumed a role of leadership through professional organizations and links to external efforts such as boards, companies, or research enterprises. Many tenured faculty would welcome an opportunity to serve on your organization in an advisory capacity, in part because it helps their post tenure review. The importance and role of "service" tends to increase over research for these faculty. They become chairs of their departments, heads of degrees, program directors, and the like. This means their time may be more limited, but their willingness to partner increased. They may also have the ability to link the projects to needed resources (students, labs, etc.) more easily. Further, projects that raise their or their unit's or institution's profile are desired and are important accomplishments to point to during their annual review. Research labs, executive training, and keynote speaking at events all create useful accomplishment points in the path toward promotion for these faculty and again, are the reasons they would take your call.

Illustrations have been created especially for this book by Charles Larson.

Pre-Tenure (Tenure-Track) Faculty

These faculty typically engage in a mix of teaching, research, and service activities and will commonly have the title "Assistant Professor". Tenure-track faculty may be interested in engaging with you depending on the level of funded research they are already doing.

> For tenure-track faculty, the most attractive thing about you is your data (sorry), and the potential external funding and associated publications that you may bring for which they may get credit – externally funded and published research is the "coin of the realm" on the tenure track.

When a faculty is hired, they start a "tenure clock" – typically six years – to "prove" that they will be able to sustain funding and publication. At most institutions one to two high quality publications (generally defined as the 'impact factor', acceptance rate, or citations to the journal) a year suffices but may be more depending on the field and the institution. "Very High Research Activity" institutions – like Drexel University or the University of Michigan – often place a premium on publishing productivity because they are measured on that productivity which in turn affects their research portfolios and of course their ability to generate funding. Be aware that pre-tenure, tenure-track faculty may be advised not to engage in external relationships at this point in their career to protect their time and ensure they are publishing.

Non-Tenure Track Faculty

You may hear terms like "Professor of the Practice", "Clinical Appointment", "Teaching Faculty", or "Lecturer". These titles generally describe faculty – who may or may not have a PhD, with limited expectations to generate external funding, research or publication. Their primary role within an analytics or data science program is to teach. As a result, their interests in collaborating with you are typically aligned with student projects, practicums and maybe guest lectures.

> Faculty think of "guest lecturers" in the same way we think about taking the kids to the grandparents – everyone gets a break.

Research Faculty

Research faculty are common at large research universities like the University of Michigan – they may opt for or a position where research funds part or all of their salary and they must offset their salary with external funds. Or, for some, they obtain a grant or project which "buys out" some of their 1/8s of time otherwise dedicated to teaching. This is sometimes an option for partnering with a university if you feel your project needs a specific faculty's expertise. This will require funding typically at some percentage of the faculty person's full salary and benefits. How much time you might need from them will also be an issue. In our case, if we think of eighths, you can break that down into workable hours. For our University a one unit buy-out is roughly 12% of their salary plus "fringe". Fringe benefit rates can run typically in the 20% to 40% range of total salary and include any non-salary benefits the employees receives such as retirement contributions, health and other insurance, or leave benefits. Research faculty, because of the demands of research grants, have less ability to partner – unless your company is the sponsor of the research grant. Federal rules around supplemental forms of income do not allow for their time to be spent outside of the grants they have, if federally sponsored (i.e., through the National Science Foundation or the National Institutes of Health). It is also true that many universities do not support payment to faculty in excess of their eight units of work. More recently, universities have begun to look at the broader impacts of research and service, which often have blurry edges. This is important and relevant to you because you need to position a project to ensure that the process and/or outcomes is of maximum benefit and alignment to the needs of the faculty while also serving the needs of your organization.

For most faculty, one of the biggest incentives to work with you is related to the types of students they work with. If they mentor doctoral students (see Chapter 5), they will be laser focused on ensuring adequate funding to ensure these students do not starve (really – doctoral students need a lot of care and feeding). They may also be seeking data sources to test and validate student research – note that this could be particularly unique opportunity to test your data with cutting edge research/algorithms. The legal challenges here can be deep, but with an understanding of the advantages and property rights for all parties, the issues can usually be addressed. If the faculty are working with master's level students, they will be interested in some combination of internships and capstone projects, and possibly sponsorship of a thesis. These initiatives are mutually beneficial and can provide a company with access to new knowledge and a pipeline of more qualified practitioners, which is especially helpful in fields like analytics and data science (see Chapter 4). If faculty are working with undergraduate students (see Chapter 3), the emphasis will likely be on internships, practicums, and hackathons, which are more exposure-based and can provide a company with a period of useful labor, but also a pipeline for entry level positions.

Table 2.4 summarizes how faculty at differing academic ranks – in ascending order of seniority – may think about collaborating with companies.

Each of these themes will re-emerge in the following chapters when we discuss the types of programs and student interactions you may have.

A View from the Ground

The following is a view of working with universities from the perspective of a senior data scientist. If you are new to collaborations, you may find this account useful when considering your own needs, or if you have worked with universities in the past, you may find these reflections a good comparator.

Table 2.4 Faculty Rank, Tenure Status, and Incentives for Corporate Collaborations

Academic Rank	Tenure Status	Faculty Incentives for Collaboration
Lecturer/Professor of the Practice or Clinical Faculty	Non-Tenure Track (often no PhD)	No research or publication requirements. Primary incentive for collaboration is in-class speaking and capstone project sponsorship. These faculty are almost exclusively aligned with undergraduate programs ("Clinical Faculty" or "Professor of the Practice" may be aligned with the Business School, i.e., the MBA Program).
Assistant Professor	Non-Tenure Track (PhD)	No research or publication requirements. Primary incentive for collaboration is in-class speaking and capstone project sponsorship. These faculty are almost exclusively aligned with undergraduate programs.
Assistant Professor	Tenure Track	Heavy emphasis on research and publication. Sponsored research (with the opportunity to publish) would be the strongest incentive. These faculty may work with students at the undergraduate or master's levels.
Associate Professor	Tenured	Combination of research, innovation, consulting, community engagement, and student capstone project sponsorship. If the faculty is working on a federally funded grant, they may not be available to work with any other partners. These faculty may work with students at any level. If they have a strong research orientation, they will be aligned with a doctoral program.
Professor	Tenured	Consulting. Potentially sponsored research. Community engagement. These faculty may work with students at any level.

Khalifeh Al-Jadda, Director of Data Science, The Home Depot

Data science as an emerging field has been one of the most challenging areas of recruitment for all companies. However, due to the significant impact data science teams have made in their companies and the great ROI in this area in many companies, most business leaders and executives see the value in investing in data science. Therefore, many companies turn to universities as an important source of talented recruits for data science teams. The unique thing about data science is how close it brings the industry and research communities to work with each other since research skills are essential in any successful data science organization. That said, any successful data science team in industry relies on hiring graduate students from research labs that actively work on data science areas like machine learning, computer vision, deep learning, NLP, etc.

During my tenure as a data science leader in different companies, I have established different forms of collaboration with universities, which helped me to achieve great things that cannot be accomplished without those partnerships.

These forms of collaboration include serving on advisory board of data science programs at universities to establishing internship programs focused on research and development. Below, I highlight my experience in different forms of collaboration with universities.

Internships

> One of the most successful hiring strategies in data science is the internship.

I personally started my career in data science as an intern at CareerBuilder which gave me exposure to solving real-life problems and working on large scale datasets at the enterprise level. After I become a data science leader and hiring manager, I started to leverage the internship as an exploration arm of my teams. We hire PhD/MSc students every semester based on their research background then we assign them a research/discovery project to work on for three months while one of the full-time data scientists within the team mentors them. Those interns in turn contribute significantly to our exploration effort by building POCs during their internship using cutting-edge techniques and new models that we have yet to explore as a team due to our busy schedule maintaining and optimizing existing models that power our production environment. On the other hand, such internship programs contribute significantly to our portfolio of patents and research papers which play an important role in attracting top talents to join our teams.

Here is a list of benefits that I believe a strong data science internship program can bring to any data science leader:

1. Discover new talented recruits for the full-time opportunities and avoid any false-positive hiring.
2. Explore new models and techniques to solve challenging problems.
3. Enrich the team's portfolio of publications and patents.
4. Reduce the cost of research projects incurred by contracting with outside firms.

Research Collaboration

Another interesting form of collaboration is in Research. In this form of collaboration, we find a research lab that works on one of the challenging problems that we would like to solve for our company. Therefore, we offer financial support to that research lab either as a gift or as a scholarship to one or two of the graduate students of that research lab then we start working with the professor and graduate students in that research lab on our own dataset so as to leverage their techniques and algorithms on our datasets to solve one of our challenging problems. This form of collaboration is usually a long-term investment where we work with the research lab for six months to a year or more, and solve challenging problems at a large scale, which cannot be solved using a single intern over a semester (e.g., building knowledge graphs or deep learning frameworks). However, the data science leaders must always be careful since such collaboration will require companies to compromise their IP rules and be willing to give up (or at least share) any patents that come out of such collaboration. Moreover, there is a risk that such collaboration may not have any direct impact on the business since some research labs tend to focus on the research side of the work instead of the applicability and scalability of their solutions.

The pros and cons of a research collaboration:

1. Produces high quality research which usually contributes significantly to the organization's portfolio of industry thought leadership and patents.
2. Solves challenging problems at a large scale.
3. Allows flexibility since the research lab will have access to the company's data and they will work in the lab according to their own schedule.

4. Saves the cost of hosting the researchers in the company's office.
5. Risks not having a direct impact at the end of the contract.
6. Requires companies to compromise their IP rules and give up some patent rights.

Advisory Board Membership

I served on the Board of Directors of the Analytics and Data Science Institute at Kennesaw State University. This unique experience gave me a chance to have a closer look at the challenges that face data science educators. Before joining that advisory board, I wasn't aware of the lack of funding that such programs face to attract faculty members with the right research background to keep up with the industry needs. On the other hand, as an industry leader I was able to share industry expectations from the graduates of such programs, what are the core skills that we care about and the research areas in highest demand. Moreover, being on that board of directors gave me an opportunity to work closely with the professors and instructors to share some of the industry use cases and recent work so the students can prepare themselves for the transition from research labs to industry.

Overall, serving on an advisory board:

1. Makes you more keenly aware of the challenges that face the data science programs at universities and can try to help solve some of those challenges.
2. Bridges the gap between industry and academia by sharing the expectations and core skills needed in the industry to help those who run the data science programs in universities focus on those skills.
3. Helps students to understand the difference between the research projects in their labs and the practical data science projects in companies.

Our Summary Checklist for Working with Universities

For any manager of an analytical organization interested in approaching a university for the purposes of recruiting talent, establishing a pipeline for talent, sponsoring a capstone course or project, collaborating in research, or executive education, we have provided a checklist to get started. As you think about what you want out of a university engagement, we have provided more specific checklists in the succeeding chapters. As a starting point, consider

- ✓ Be clear on what you and your organization are expecting to get out of the relationship.
- ✓ Why do you want to partner with *this* university? Have the graduates from this university been successful at your organization? Are there particular faculty members that produce research or teach courses that are well aligned with your organizational objectives?
- ✓ Develop an understanding of why the university and/or faculty would want to collaborate with you and your organization. Remember that different types of faculty have different incentive systems depending on where they are in their career. They need to have a reason to return your call. Funding is important, but not sufficient.
- ✓ Understand that one size does not fit all. Companies with a successful history of university collaborations typically have a portfolio of university relationships.
- ✓ Consider your appetite for sharing intellectual property and publication of research findings. For research faculty and most pre-tenure/tenure-track faculty this will not only be a priority but if there is no appetite at your organization for sharing intellectual property, the faculty will be dis-incented from working with you.
- ✓ If your organizational priorities are particularly related to hiring entry level talent, consider partnering with strong undergraduate and regional institutions, which may be easier to "navigate". In addition, there are broader latent "community-based" benefits to hiring locally. Alternatively, if your priorities are related to research, consider reaching out to large research universities with centers and institutes.

Endnotes

1. Industry-University Cooperative Research Centers (IUCRC), National Science Foundation. https://iucrc.nsf.gov/ Accessed June 10, 2020.
2. The Carnegie Classifications of Institutions of Higher Learning. https://carnegieclassifications.iu.edu/lookup/lookup.php Accessed April 20, 2020.
3. Colleges that Change Lives. https://ctcl.org/category/college-profiles/ Accessed June 10, 2020.
4. Association to Advance Collegiate Business Schools. https://www.aacsb.edu/ Accessed June 3, 2020.
5. Accreditation Board for Engineering and Technology. https://www.abet.org/ Accessed June 3, 2020.
6. Drexel University. https://drexel.edu/provost/policies/faculty_workload/ Accessed April 13, 2020.

Chapter 3

Collaborating with Undergraduate Programs

What Do Undergraduates Really Know?

If you are reading this, you probably completed an undergraduate degree in something, at some point (this was longer ago for some than it was for others). Looking back, you likely recall at least three things about your undergraduate experience: you did not really get into your "major" until your junior (3rd) year, you did not know as much as you think you did (the hubris of youth), and students who took the time to get an internship or engage in a co-op were more likely to get a good job.

These three points are interconnected.

Let's start by addressing why you likely took classes in the first two years in subjects that you may or may not have sought out.

Almost 95% of all U.S. colleges and universities use an academic calendar with two primary 15-week semesters – Fall and Spring – with an 8-week summer semester[1]. Most undergraduate programs have a stated requirement of approximately 120–130 credit hours of study to earn a bachelor's degree[2] which equates to approximately 40 courses (most undergraduate courses are 3 credit hours). Credit hour requirements for a few common majors can be found in Figure 3.1.

The average number of credit hours actually earned by undergraduate students is closer to 135. In fact, only about 40% of students enrolled in a four-year college program graduate in four years[3] (make a note of this for when your child starts college). There are several reasons for the extra time/credit hours, including changing school, changing major, failed classes, and, of course the catchall category of "life events".

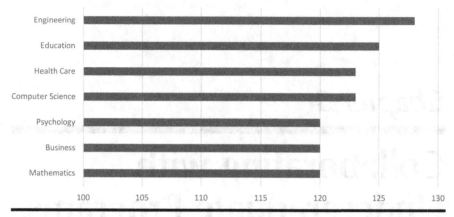

Figure 3.1 Average required credit hours for selected undergraduate major in the United States (2018).

Across all undergraduate degrees offered through universities and colleges in the United States, there are roughly three categories of courses: general education, major required courses, and electives. See Figure 3.2.

So, what exactly happens in each of those three sections and, as an analytics professional trying to engage with a university, why should you care?

The bulk of most undergraduate degrees in the United States stems from a strong emphasis on liberal arts foundations. Historically, the goal of the liberal arts education was to provide a general framework of knowledge, exposure to a breadth of subjects to promote critical thinking, and to be a bridge to higher level curriculums in applied fields of study. However, the number of strictly "liberal arts" colleges in the United States has declined precipitously with an associated rise in more technical colleges[4]. Despite this drop in entire curriculums being liberal arts based,

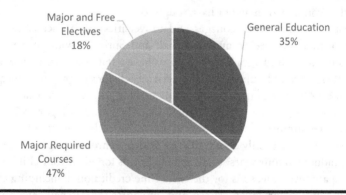

Figure 3.2 Typical distribution of undergraduate credit hours in the United States.

most bachelor's degree programs have some number of credits required in general education which are typically split among humanities, social sciences, mathematics, writing, the arts, history, and physical, environmental, chemical, and/or biological sciences. While the total number of credits vary by institution, it is usually about one third of all required credit hours (see Figure 3.1). Beyond that, students have requirements for their majors, which often reflect some notion of required competency needed as directed by the field's accrediting body. For example, a nurse would need so many instructional hours and clinical hours across directed subjects and still need to pass a competency exam to gain a practice license at the level of Registered Nurse (RN). Similarly, an engineering student in an accredited program must take two or three semesters of general education, followed by two semesters of mathematics and science and at least three semesters of instruction in engineering courses – and then pass two competency exams to apply for licensure as a practicing engineer. Other fields have similar requirements (e.g., education, accounting). After general education and major course work, any remaining credit hours are "electives" – courses open to student choice.

It is worth noting that there is no standardized curriculum – or governing body – for data science.

The key message here is that whether a student is studying nursing, engineering, or data science, the material is still relatively "high level" and theoretical. General education courses are effectively introductory survey courses. This means that higher level learning opportunities are limited at the bachelor's level – by design. What is emphasized is the critical thinking involved and hopefully holistic view of how subjects, theories, and phenomena intersect into higher level models of inquiry. In other words, at the undergraduate level, students are really "learning how to learn".

In the last year of study, undergraduate students increasingly participate in some type of internship or capstone experience (*when they make us the benevolent dictators of education, we would require that all students graduating from an accredited university in the 21st century would have an internship or capstone experience... but we digress...*). Capstone courses and internships have been identified as "high-impact" educational practices – those practices having the greatest contribution to a successful undergraduate experience (i.e., degree completion, employment in field of choice). The American Association of Colleges and Universities identified High-Impact Educational Practices[5] as:

■ Common Intellectual Experiences
■ Learning Communities

- Writing-Intensive Courses
- Collaborative Assignments and Projects
- Undergraduate Research
- Diversity/Global Learning
- Service Learning
- Community-Based Learning
- **Capstone Courses**
- **Internships**

These practices – which again are increasingly integrated into undergraduate programs across the United States – are high impact because they require students to do (at least) four things:

- High-impact practices demand that students devote considerable time and effort to purposeful tasks and require regular decisions that deepen their involvement as well as their commitment to their academic program and to their college.
- They help students build substantive relationships by requiring them to interact with faculty and peers about complex, integrated matters over extended periods of time. As professors with almost 50 collective years of teaching experience (Bob is older), it continues to amaze us how few students actually interact with faculty outside the classroom. We don't bite – at least not hard.
- They challenge students to work with students from other disciplines and other backgrounds and contribute to new ways of thinking about and responding to novel circumstances as they work on intellectual and practical tasks, inside and outside the classroom, on and off campus. From your own experience, consider how many times – particularly in the later years of your program – you worked with students who were majoring in a discipline different from your own. Historically, students were rarely provided the opportunity to collaborate with students or faculty outside of their discipline. However, today most work is done in collaborative teams comprised of people with different skills and typically different types of formalized training. This is particularly true and relevant for data science, where almost all work is done in teams of specialists.
- They help students apply and test what they are learning in new situations. High-impact practices provide opportunities for students to see how what they are learning works in different settings and create contexts to integrate, synthesize, and apply knowledge.

Long-standing, well-established undergraduate programs of study have had to retro-actively integrate high-impact practices into their curricula. However, the first generation of undergraduate programs in data science have been able to integrate these high-impact practices into their curricula from the beginning. As an analytics manager looking for opportunities to work with an undergraduate population, understand that capstone courses, internships, and applied project opportunities are the "ultimate" examples of high impact educational experiences.

While an applied data project is an effective way for you and your organization to evaluate and recruit students for positions, note that these types of engagements make an important contribution to the students' educational experience. In addition, faculty within these undergraduate programs are likely regularly on the lookout for corporate partners to help develop and structure these projects – so you are also helping to "lighten the load" for a lecturer or assistant professor who may be scrambling to meet their course requirements.

The Rise of Undergraduate Data Science Programs

Unlike most academic fields, data science did not begin as an undergraduate discipline – but rather as a fundamentally master's-level discipline with heavy emphasis on application. As the evolution of data created unprecedented opportunities and challenges for all sectors of the economy, master's-level programs with heavy emphasis on analytics and predictive modeling began emerging in 2006. Doctoral programs with emphasis on innovation and research first emerged in 2015. While most students who ultimately pursued a master's or doctoral degree in data science studied mathematics, statistics, computer science, or engineering, colleges and universities began offering formal bachelor's-level programs in the field in 2018. Over the past several years, undergraduate programs in data science have emerged at colleges and universities at all levels across the country[6]. These undergraduate programs aim to fill a niche between less technically demanding "business analyst" programs offered by business departments and more technically demanding, but typically less applied, mathematics, computer science, and statistics programs.

> Most undergraduate programs in data science focus on producing graduates who possess a high level of mathematical and statistical expertise, programming skills in several languages, a basic background in computer science, and a healthy sense of how to use their technical skillset to solve real-world business problems.

Bachelor's-level programs present analytics managers with opportunities for fruitful engagement, and they may be underleveraged by the business community given the relative newness of bachelor's degrees in the field.

As noted above, unlike engineering, computer science, or accounting, data science does not have an accrediting body or nationally standardized curriculum (the Certified Analytics Professional or "CAP" credential offered through the organization Institute for Operations Research and the Management Sciences (INFORMS) is gaining recognition but is not a curricular credentialing body (see Chapter 6)). While there are some common courses to be found in almost all data science programs (e.g., machine learning, programming, predictive analytics, database structures), programs across the country continue to exhibit variation in expectations related to mathematics, programming languages, and areas of application. These differences are largely a function of where the program is housed. Programs in data science can by housed in the College of Computing, the College of Science, the College of Engineering, the Business School, or in a "neutral" center or institute.

> It might be useful to think about the discipline of data science like tofu – the core protein is the same, but the flavors will be different depending upon the preparation.

Staying with this analogy, an undergraduate data science program housed in a College of Business may require many of the same courses as a program housed in the College of Computing – but they will have very different "flavors" at the end – making for two very different recruiting targets.

> It can be a very confusing hiring market when students with the same degree – data science – have different non-standardized skills; communications, modeling, and programming are all important skills for data science students, but students' strengths and weaknesses will vary depending if they are studying in the business college, the college of computing or somewhere in between.

This is a critical concept for analytical managers working with universities to fully understand and appreciate. Consider three very different undergraduate degrees in data science highlighted in Table 3.1.

Three of the early formal undergraduate degrees in data science programs are housed at the College of Charleston[7], the University of Georgia[8], and the University of New Hampshire[9]. These universities each have well architected curriculums in data science and reflect many of the high-impact educational practices listed above. It is worth noting that the University of Georgia and the University of New Hampshire are both classified as "Doctoral University: Very High Research

Table 3.1 Comparison of Three Undergraduate Data Science Programs

	College of Charleston	*University of Georgia*	*University of New Hampshire*
Academic Location	School of Science and Mathematics	College of Arts and Sciences (Department of Statistics)	College of Engineering and Physical Science (Department of Computer Science)
Total Number of Required Credit Hours	122	120	128
Noteworthy Courses	Students are required to have an area of emphasis for their electives (business, science, social science, arts, and humanities)	Students must take a course in data security and privacy. Elective option in Computing Ethics and Society	Students are required to take a four-credit-hour course in Professional and Technical Writing
Internship/ Capstone Requirements	Capstone course required	Capstone course required, plus internship elective	Students must take a capstone course, the internship preparedness course, and a three-credit internship

Activity", while the College of Charleston is classified as "Master's College and University" (see Table 2.1).

For analytics managers who may be interested in collaborating with any of these three programs (they are all excellent), they should consider where these programs are housed within the respective universities; while all three programs have many of the same courses, the academic location will influence the different skills, strengths, and weaknesses of the students.

Views from the Ground

Dr. Jeremiah Johnson, Co-Director for the B.S. Data Science Program at the University of New Hampshire, has worked with undergraduate students for over 10 years. Below, he shares his perspectives on the unique issues and opportunities for engaging undergraduate data science programs in either capstone courses or internships.

> First and foremost, in order to get the most out of engagement with undergraduate populations, it is important to consider *why* the students are interested in the engagement (beyond the program requirement).

> The best outcomes tend to occur when both the student's and the company's interests align.

Just like their graduate student counterparts (see Chapter 4), undergraduate students are primarily seeking "real-world" experience, with an eye toward improving their prospects on the job market postgraduation. While some students may have an interest in a master's or doctoral degree, most are planning on entering the job market immediately after graduation. The student will want to build a portfolio of work, and to begin establishing their network of contacts. Given these objectives, a manager seeking to engage with an undergraduate population should ask the following questions:

■ Will this engagement provide the student with practical, "real-world" experience?
■ Will this engagement provide the student with a concrete contribution to their portfolio of work?
■ Will this engagement enable the student to begin developing their professional network?
■ Is the company interested in recruiting talented students at the bachelor level?

Even if the answer to the last question is "no", there may still be benefit to the company in engaging with undergraduate students – a student who has a successful internship experience at a company that only hires for data science roles at the master's or PhD level may then pursue an advanced degree with an aspiration toward a permanent position at the company. A middle way that can benefit both the company and the university is to hire post-baccalaureates contingent on completion of the requisite advanced degree, perhaps with company support provided for the student as they complete the degree. Think of this like developing a "farm team" for your major league operation.

While both capstone courses and internships are high-impact educational experiences, there are significant differences which need to be appreciated to ensure success. In particular, internship work typically takes place at the company, under the primary supervision of a manager. Capstone project work, on the other hand, typically is done at the student's university, under the guidance and primary supervision of a faculty mentor (see Table 3.2). Critically, both should start with a meaningful, non-trivial project of some relevance to the organization.

For a full-time undergraduate student, an internship or capstone project is likely to be but one of three or four courses that the student is taking. This means that often the scope of work that an undergraduate can undertake will be less than that able to be undertaken by a graduate student over a comparable timeframe. For instance, an undergraduate student completing a for-credit hour internship will

Table 3.2 Distinctions Between Internships and Capstones

	Internship	Capstone
Year of Program	Typically 3rd, but can be taken from the 2nd year	Final year
Location	On company site	On campus
Timing	Often summer, but can occur any time during the academic year	Typically during the fall or spring semester
Primary Mentor	Company manager	University faculty member
Provides College/ University Credit	Typically, but not always	Yes
Paid	If credit hours are earned for the internship, it is less likely to be paid. Credit hours are a form of "currency"	No
Collection of Students	Typically completed as an individual student working with a supervisor	Frequently completed as a class with other students working under a faculty mentor. The class may include students from multiple disciplines working in teams

typically be required to complete at least 150 hours of work during the course of the internship. These hours may need to be verified by an internship coordinator at the university. If the internship responsibilities are not expected to be completed over a standard 15-week semester, then the student should be expected to work ten hours per week on average, and the project to which the student is assigned should be chosen with that level of commitment in mind.

It is reasonable to expect that when you engage with an undergraduate population via an internship or capstone project, the level of difficulty or complexity of the proposed project will need to be substantially reduced from that expected of graduate students. This is true because a graduate student in data science has already completed a bachelor's degree, and regardless of their undergraduate field of study has therefore gone through four (or more) years of an educational program that, at a minimum, grants them a certain level of maturity that may not yet be present in an undergraduate student. This will manifest, for example, in ways such as improved time management skills, communication skills, and overall comfort working in a professional environment. However, it can be said with some certainty that by the time an undergraduate student is ready for an internship or capstone project, the student has spent a substantial amount of time in their program (two years at a minimum) establishing a strong technical foundation, and this may enable them to exceed expectations. For example, students in our Bachelor of Science program in Analytics & Data Science are required to complete both an internship **and** a capstone project for the degree. This internship usually takes place over the summer between the student's third and fourth years of study. At this point in the program, the student will have taken mathematics courses including applied linear algebra and calculus-based statistics. They will have learned to program in multiple programming languages, including Python, R, SAS, and C++, and they will be familiar with SQL and relational databases. Finally, they will have completed two specialized, project-based applied data science courses that integrate their technical skillset into a cohesive data analysis pipeline. This prepares them to handle a large swath of typical analytics tasks from the first day that they step into the workplace.

Given all of this, where might they come up short? Well, the average student will be very new to streaming and unstructured data. In our program, they would not have been exposed to some of the more sophisticated modeling techniques commonly used in some contexts, such as deep learning or gradient boosting. They likely will not yet have been exposed to specialized tools and techniques for working with large, unstructured datasets, and streaming data.

Structuring Successful Internships

As a high-impact practice, internships are a common requirement in many undergraduate programs besides data science, and there are common aspects to all successful internships. Any internship program should prepare the student for success after the internship is completed. The training that undergraduate students in data science undertake in the first few years of their program is broadly dispersed between mathematics, statistics, and computer science. This means that when it comes to structuring internships for data science students, there are many potential types of projects where a student can make a meaningful contribution. For example, in our program, several students have had successful internships in what are probably best described as "data-centric software engineering" roles, focused on tasks such as building databases to integrate and clean up company data. Other students have focused on predictive modeling. As an example, one student from our program recently completed a successful internship developing predictive models for insurance data using neural networks. A key contributor to the success of an internship is ensuring the suitability of the chosen role for the students: the student working in the "data engineering" role was one of our strongest programmers, with excellent software development skills, while the student working in the "data science" role building neural networks came in with a deeper than average mathematics background that prepared him to take a role building sophisticated models before he had been thoroughly trained in them through our curriculum. It perhaps goes without saying that managers should seek interns with the right skills for the job; although all undergraduates in analytics and data science go through the same coursework and develop a similar skillset, some will be more suited for some roles than others.

Keep in mind that from the student's perspective, accomplishing the technical aspects of the project are only a part of the overall objective. The best student internship experiences will provide opportunities for the student to network and establish contacts in the field, as well as to present their work and build a portfolio that they can share as evidence of work accomplished. Such opportunities are especially important in the field of data science and should be a part of any internship experience.

Structuring Successful Capstones

The capstone project is often the final requirement in an undergraduate degree program. The biggest difference between the two is that capstones are commonly offered as "courses" with 10–20 students working together, while internships are commonly offered to an individual student who will work independently under the supervision of a faculty member. As with internships, there are common best practices for capstone courses that analytics managers seeking university relationships should consider. For the student, the capstone project course should provide an opportunity to demonstrate both the breadth and the depth of their newly acquired skillset. Because the capstone is overseen by faculty and work is primarily done on campus, this requires the manager to be able to essentially hand off the project for a period of time (10–15 weeks for a standard 15-week semester) while the students work under the guidance of their faculty mentor. There needs to be clear communication between the manager, the faculty overseeing the capstone, and the students. The manager must have a certain degree of confidence in the faculty mentor who will oversee the project. Given the degree of separation between the manager and the students, the project needs to be clearly delineated. What are the objectives? What are the deliverables? What is the timetable to completion? What data is needed? Who will provide the data, and how will it be managed? All of these questions and more need to be carefully thought through when planning a capstone.

High Impact in Action – Two Case Studies

Jeremiah shared an internship case study from the B.S. in Data Science Program at the University of New Hampshire. He provides context from the perspectives of the student, the university and of the sponsoring organization.

In the Spring of 2020, a third-year data science student interned at a local startup company specializing in in autonomous systems, unmanned aerial vehicles (UAVs), drones, and counter-unmanned aircraft systems (CUAS). The company's products included an intelligence analysis software based on telemetry data that determines a UAV's payload deployment, threat assessments, anomaly detection, FAA compliance, mission profiling, geo-fence violation, and rollover detection. The student's role was to develop several classification models related to product performance over a 15-week period (one semester). An example of the student's project included developing a classification model to determine if an unmanned system travels in a straight line for the majority of the flight path. For this project, the student had to use the Pandas, NumPy, and Matplotlib libraries within Jupyter Notebook to analyze the latitude and longitude values within an unmanned system flight path. The student also had to work with other unique data, such as UTC timestamps and battery voltages while using GitHub for code revision over several development iterations.

During the three months of the onsite internship, the student attended daily staff meetings, biweekly check-in meetings with the director of engineering, and monthly staff meetings, where the CEO and COO would update the staff and contractors regarding company accolades, developments in their market, and future plans.

The internship was successful and mutually beneficial for both student and company. The aspects of the internship that contributed to success include:

- The objectives of the student project were clearly defined, with a detailed calendar of weekly expectations and deliverables.
- While the student had limited domain knowledge (few undergraduates will have any industry knowledge when they begin an internship), he was well versed in the data science-dimensions of the project and was highly proficient in the programming languages required.
- The student had a direct supervisor for the duration of the project who provided feedback and mentoring (and infinite patience).

- Through staff meetings, the student was able to engage with other employees, senior leaders, and other parts of the organization, which allowed him to better understand the organizational culture.
- The project was substantive and relevant to the business – it was not "busywork".

The second undergraduate case study highlights an applied project course. This case study comes from Dr. Riaan De Jongh, Director of the Centre for Business Mathematics and Informatics at North-West University in South Africa.

When students arrive at the university for their first year of study, they have a vague idea about the problems or tasks they will encounter in their professional careers. Frequently students enquire about the type of problems they will face one day, and how the course/modules they are taking will assist them in solving these problems. To give them a flavor of what they could encounter in practice, a first-year course was designed with the main objective to expose the student to a purposefully vague financial problem statement (provided by a large regional bank), which they have to formulate and then solve using a combination of mathematics and computer programming. In the process, the students should experience initial bewilderment and the pain of not knowing where to start. They should realize upfront that they do not yet have the necessary knowledge and are not able to ask the right questions to formulate the problem. Then the students are taken through a process of acquiring the relevant knowledge which will eventually enable them to ask the right questions to formulate the problem in mathematical terms. Once this is achieved the student is required to derive the mathematical solution to the problem and translate it into an algorithm that can be programmed. Part of the process involves confronting the student with other questions relevant to the problem at hand. In this way the student explores other facets of the problem that increase the functionality of the decision support system they have to design, develop, and present to the sponsoring financial institution. Although the students have the benefit of the lecturer's guidance on the financial concepts, the various problems to be addressed, the associated mathematical formulations and resulting equations, very little guidance is given on the design of the decision support system and the associated programming requirements. The case study addresses all the ingredients of a typical data science project, albeit without the typical large data set, which they will experience in later, more advanced courses. The course requires students to integrate mathematical problem formulation, computer programming, creative thinking, project management, system design and development, and presentation skills. A "typical" course problem:

1. **Initial problem statement**
   Your fellow student would like to prepare for retirement, and you need to advise him how he should plan for this. In order to do proper financial consulting, you have to design and build a decision support system. Questions that your fellow student could ask includes, but are not limited

to: How much money should I set aside now and until my retirement, on a monthly basis, to ensure that I will make adequate provision for my retirement?

2. **Detailed problem formulation**

   After your interview with the student, you have the following information:
   - The nominal interest rate.
   - Initial investment amount and regular deposit schedule.
   - Assumptions regarding inflation.
   - Timing and size of withdrawals.

   With the information provided, calculate the value of the first payment at the end of January 2021. Develop an excel sheet where you can illustrate the effect on the first payment when there are changes in the input parameters. Draw graphs to illustrate this. What parameters have the greatest influence on the initial payment? Will you be able to handle once-off payments and/or withdrawals by the student? Think about the functionality you would like to build in your decision support system.

3. **Mathematical formulation**

   Formulate the requirements mathematically. Test the formulas and report the results.

4. **Decision support system**

   Your decision support system should at least be able to solve the mathematical formulation but should be flexible enough to answer most of the problems that you had to solve in this module. Although you have done most of the practical work in MS Excel, you may use any programming language to develop your system; for example, Python, Visual Basic, C##, R, SAS or any other programming language you are comfortable with. You may even consider developing an application in Apple IOS or Android. The most important thing is that you use your creative thinking ability to come up with a system that is able to address all sorts of other questions. Consider some of the questions we asked you in the exams and assignments. Would your system be able to solve these? Examples of typical questions are given below.

Question 1:

i. For three months the monthly effective interest rate is 0.90% per month. It is followed by a nominal interest rate of 8.8% per year, compounded quarterly for the following nine months. Calculate the equivalent continuous interest rate over the period.

ii. For six months the interest rate is 8.5% per year. It is followed by an interest rate of 4.6% effective per half-year, for the following year and a half. Calculate the equivalent nominal interest rate, compounded monthly, over the period.

Question 2:

On 1 July 2018, Gianni opens a savings account and starts to invest an amount of money at the end of each month into the savings account. The first investment is $150 and will increase every month thereafter with 0.7%. He plans on making these investments for a total of seven years. On 1 January 2021, Gianni decides that for the next three and a half years he will make an additional constant investment of X at the start of every quarter into the savings account. The savings account earns interest at 6.8% per year, compounded quarterly. Calculate the total present value of all the investments in the bank account on 1 January 2017.

Question 3:

A young couple decides to buy a house for $100,000. They plan on paying 15% of the purchase price immediately as a deposit. The remaining balance of the purchase price will be financed by a bank loan that will be repaid over a period of 20 years. They agree to repay the bank as follows:

- For the first 10 years, they will pay an amount of Y at the end of each month.
- For the remaining 10 years, they will pay an amount of 3Y at the end of each quarter.

The interest rate is constant at 3.5% per year.

i. Calculate Y.

ii. Calculate the interest and capital component of the 121st payment.

5. **Final deliverable**

Students must develop a deployable decision support system. An example of the front end of such a student's final deliverable is presented in Figure 3.3. The decision support system is characterized by many functions including, but not limited to:

- Conversion of interest rates,
- Present and future value of annuities (investments and loan amortization),
- Changing inputs, e.g., interest rates, inflation, investment payment or withdrawal, lump sum investments and withdrawals, date and time of investment/withdrawal,
- Retirement planning,
- Comparing and adding retirement planning scenarios.

The system depicted in Figure 3.3 supports the ability to solve all three questions.

This applied project course at North-West University is regularly over-enrolled and is one of the more popular courses on campus, with many students ultimately working for the banking institutions that provide problems for the course. Students eventually take a more advanced capstone course at the end of their program, which

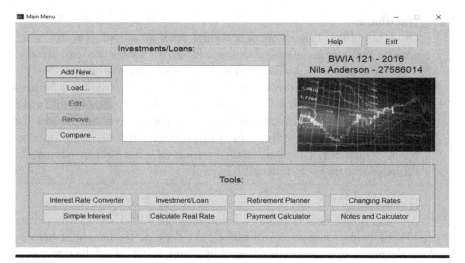

Figure 3.3 Example of undergraduate data science students' decision support system.

builds on the "high impact" practices from this first-year project course. The specific aspects of this course that contribute to its ongoing success include:

- The professor has a long, successful track record of teaching the course and helping students with placement after graduation. As a result, he, and other lecturers that present the course from time to time, have a strong reputation and credibility within the local business community. They understand the needs and "language" of the business community and can translate this into an academic curriculum.
- While the "content" of the problem may change every semester, the course project process does not change.
- Given that this course is housed within the Business Mathematics and Informatics Centre at the University, it would be expected that the students are computationally strong. This project course emphasizes "softer skills" such as problem formulation, working in teams, communications, and presentation skills, which may not come as easily for the students.

Our Summary Checklist for Working with Undergraduate Students

If you are interested in recruiting for entry-level positions – and creating an ongoing pipeline of talent – you should make a university partnership with an undergraduate program a high priority. However, undergraduate students are different from master's and doctoral-level students. Ensuring that those differences are understood and that expectations are aligned will contribute to a more successful experience for the organization, for the student, and for the associated faculty. The primary way your organization will likely engage with undergraduate students is through internships and capstone courses. Where there are differences between the two, they share many best practices that managers seeking to work with undergraduate students should consider:

✓ Since internships and capstones are almost universally integrated into undergraduate data science programs, the instructors and program directors should welcome your offer to engage students in this context. This is a particularly strong way to start a conversation with a university for recruiting talent and building hiring pipelines, because they need your project, your data, and your agreement to engage to satisfy the requirements of the course offering.

✓ While internships and capstones benefit the university, be aware that the "higher ranked" universities may already have a long queue of companies wanting to sponsor these projects and courses. If your organization is seeking an opportunity to engage a university specifically for the objective of hiring entry-level talent (versus research, innovation, professional education), you may want to consider reaching out to a smaller, local, undergraduate institution. In addition, hiring local talent is beneficial to the community (eat local, shop local…hire local).

✓ Prior to engaging an undergraduate program, consider where the data science program is housed (e.g., Business School, Computer Science, Mathematics). Students in "data science" from the various academic units within a university will have very different strengths and weaknesses. While checking your position(s) requirements against the curriculum may be useful, a "machine learning" course in Computer Science will look very different from a "machine learning" course in a Business School.

✓ Ensure that your expectations are aligned; most undergraduate students in data science will be computationally strong but have limited (or zero) domain experience.

✓ Give undergraduate students opportunities to learn but also to have "wins" where they can apply and demonstrate their knowledge. Remember that this experience is part of their education.

✓ Internships, applied projects, and capstone courses all require a high degree of coordination between the manager, the faculty overseeing the engagement, and the students. Successful capstone courses/applied project courses may require a mentoring conversation every week in the beginning, with more mature engagements requiring conversations once a month.

✓ Factors contributing to success include well-defined, substantive content, a clear timeline, concrete deliverables, and a committed (and very patient) organizational mentor.

✓ Venues for students to present the results of their work are foundational to the engagement, because they provide the student with an opportunity to develop critical "soft skills" beyond mathematics and programming.

✓ Check sources like LinkedIn to see if alumni from this program have been recruited into your organization in the past – and if they stayed. If your organization has not hired out of this program, what types of organizations have hired these graduates? Were they start-ups? Fortune 100 corporations? How long did they stay?

Endnotes

1. National Center for Education Statistics. https://nces.ed.gov/ipeds/ Accessed May 18, 2020.
2. Nate Johnson, Leonard Reidy, Mike Droll, and R.E. LeMon (2017). Program Requirements for Associate's and Bachelor's Degrees: A National Survey https://www.insidehighered.com/sites/default/server_files/files/Program%20Requirements%20-%20A%20National%20Survey%281%29.pdf. Accessed May 18, 2020.
3. Educationdata.org. https://educationdata.org/number-of-college-graduates/#:~:text=In%20Summary%3A%2C%20and%20finally%2C%20the%20doctorate. Accessed May 17, 2020.
4. Richard H. Hersh (1997). Intention and Perceptions A National Survey of Public Attitudes Toward Liberal Arts Education, Change: The Magazine of Higher Learning, 29:2, 16–23. DOI: 10.1080/00091389709603100
5. Nancy O'Neill (2010). Internships as a High-Impact Practice: Some Reflections on Quality. https://www.aacu.org/publications-research/periodicals/internships-high-impact-practice-some-reflections-quality. Accessed May 2, 2020.
6. Data Science Community. http://datascience.community/colleges Accessed June 2, 2020.
7. College of Charleston. http://datascience.cofc.edu/ Accessed June 2, 2020.
8. University of Georgia. https://www.stat.uga.edu/data-science-major Accessed June 2, 2020.
9. University of New Hampshire. https://ceps.unh.edu/computer-science/program/bs/analytics-data-science-data-science-option Accessed June 2, 2020.

Chapter 4

Collaboration with Master's Programs

Differences Between Master's and Undergraduate Education

In the previous chapter, we discussed what organizations should and should not expect when working with undergraduate students in data science. A general summarization of undergraduate education might be that undergraduate students "learn how to learn" through a combination of general education courses, major required courses and major elective courses. Consequently, it is often the internship or capstone course – the "high-impact practices" – that uniquely enable undergraduate students to develop applied skills during their academic programs via real-world projects.

> Master's-level education might be summarized as "learning how to do what people do".

As the number and proportion of people in the United States with a bachelor's degree has increased over time, so too has the number and proportion of people with a master's degree. In 2019, 33.6% of the U.S. population over the age of 25 had earned a bachelor's degree[1]. This was up from 28% of the population in 2010 and up from just 4.6% in 1940. By 2019, approximately 10% of the U.S. population had earned a master's degree, up from just under 7% in 2010 and less than 5%

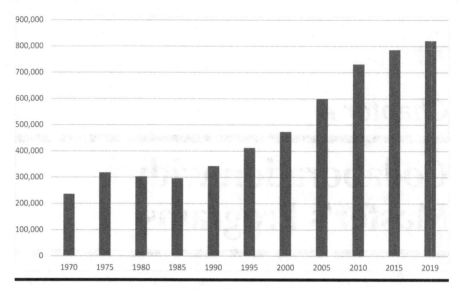

Figure 4.1 Master's degrees conferred by U.S. colleges and universities.

in 2000. The number of master's degrees conferred by U.S. academic institutions has almost doubled since 2000 and almost tripled since 1980 (see Figure 4.1)[2].

While the reasons for the increasing number of people obtaining master's degrees are varied, increased salary potential is unquestionably part of the trend. People who have master's degrees are generally paid more money than those who do not. This is true for graduates of analytics and data science programs – but potentially not at the level that you might expect. More on that later in the chapter.

The Rise of Master's Programs in Analytics and Data Science

Master's-level programs in analytics and data science formally entered the educational marketplace in 2007. In 2016, there were roughly 60 analytical master's programs, and by 2020 that number had surpassed 300 programs. See Figure 4.2. Rarely in academia has such a rapid evolution occurred – of all the things that universities are known for, quickly and efficiently responding to the needs of the marketplace has historically not been one of them. In Figure 4.2, there is a differentiation between "business analytics", "data analytics" and "data science". While some "business analytics" programs are simply repackaged MBA programs, many of these programs were purposefully architected from scratch, such as the nation's first formal analytics program at North Carolina State University through the Institute for Advanced Analytics.

Reiterating the definitions that we presented in from Chapter 1, generally, "data scientists" are considered to be a more technical subset of analytics professionals;

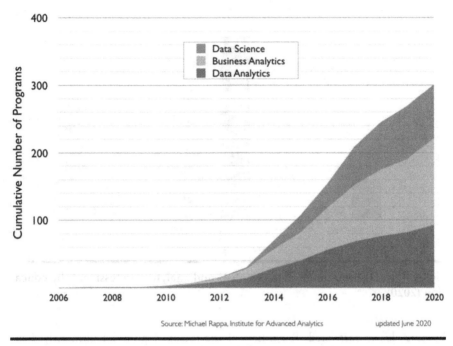

Figure 4.2 Growth of analytics and data science master's degree programs in the United States.

where analytics professionals apply a wide range of quantitative methods to derive insights and prescribe actions, data scientists will have deeper computer science skills needed to acquire, clean or transform, and model unstructured or continuously streaming data, regardless of its format, size, or source[3]. Both analytics and data science professionals are likely to have a master's degree, with data scientists equally as likely to have gone on to earn a PhD[4]. See Figure 4.3. The PhD in data science and how analytical organizations should consider engaging these doctoral programs is addressed in Chapter 5.

With this unprecedented growth in master's-level programs, it would be reasonable to question if supply is in danger of outpacing demand. Actually, demand for analytical talent and supply of analytical talent have been closely matched[5] – this is good news because unemployed alumni are not a desired outcome for any university program. See Figure 4.4. This close correlation begs the question if supply is actually *driving* demand. Given the disruptive nature of technology, the typically slower adoption of larger organizations to embed it in their workflows and the need to demonstrate value-driven use cases, this may make sense. As companies hire analytics and data science talent, the work outputs of that talent have great potential to create improved operational efficiencies. Consequently, more resources are devoted (i.e., data scientists hire more data scientists) and the supply and demand

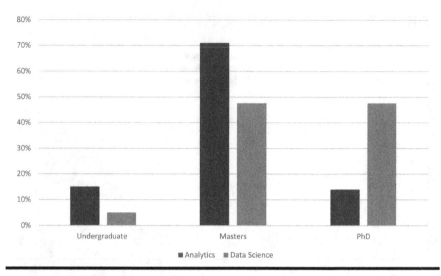

Figure 4.3 Distribution of data scientists and analytics professionals by education (2020).

become closely correlated. Regardless of the reason, Figure 4.4 ultimately demonstrates that the need for talent is still growing year over year – with the highest volume happening at the master's-level.

Salaries are also keeping pace. According to a longitudinal salary study of analytics and data science professionals, entry-level employees with an undergraduate degree in "Analytics" saw an increase in their 2020 salaries of about $2,000 after

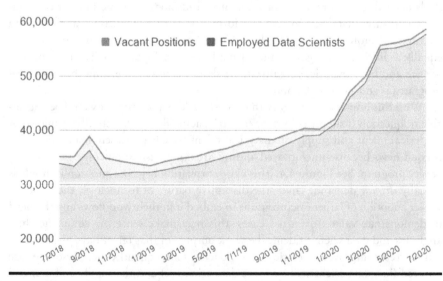

Figure 4.4 U.S. data scientists supply and vacancies – entry-level, $80K+ Salary.

Table 4.1   Distribution of Base Salaries of Analytics and Data Science Professionals in the United States by Job Level and by Education

	Analytics Professionals	*Data Science Professionals*
Entry Level		
Undergraduate	$78,615	
Master's	$80,737	$92,222
PhD	$95,778	$106,365
Managers		
Undergraduate	$127,759	
Master's	$133,483	$143,230
PhD	$138,908	$147,328

earning a MS in Analytics, and an increase of almost $15,000 when pursuing a MS in Data Science. Lower level managers – those with small teams and well-defined project scope – saw an increase of almost $6,000 after earning a MS in Analytics, and, again, about a $15,000 increase when pursuing an MS in Data Science. Again, in this context, data science professionals are generally more technical than are analytics professionals. See Table 4.1.

This proliferation of master's-trained individuals developing varying levels of expertise in analytics, data science, data engineering, predictive modeling, and machine learning has led to confusion in the hiring market for such talent and likely frustration for hiring managers when looking for talent – particularly talent with such strong salary demands.

A study completed in 2018 examined 603,424 job postings for "Analytics", "Big Data", "Business Analyst", and "Data Scientist" for the three-year period from January 2015 to December 2017[6]. While there were expected differences – with technical skills like programming and scripting languages more likely to be required for "Data Scientists" versus "Business Analysts" – there were commonalities – many positions required "communication and interpersonal" skills. See Table 4.2.

Table 4.2 summarizes the analytical skills that are in demand, but how does this compare to the "supply" of master's-level talent that is generated by universities? The same study examined what was actually being taught across 64 master's-level programs in analytics and data science in 2015. See Figure 4.5.

It is important to note that universities lean heavily into the applied project course to help master's-level students develop communications and interpersonal skills that are most in-demand across all sectors of the market and for all types of analytical positions.

Illustrations have been created especially for this book by Charles Larson.

Table 4.2 Percentage of Documents (Job Ads) that Contain at Least One Term from a Custom Topic by Job-Title Keyword (Analytics, Business Analyst, and Data Scientist)

	Analytics	Business Analyst	Data Scientist
BI software	8.00	2.86	3.80
Big data	15.12	0.89	48.53
Business domain	23.04	36.90	7.22
Business intelligence	24.23	6.38	22.51
Cloud computing	1.88	0.19	2.12
Computer science	1.93	0.05	15.66
Data handling	17.90	6.73	16.55
Database	39.77	26.03	50.18

Table 4.2   Percentage of Documents (Job Ads) that Contain at Least One Term from a Custom Topic by Job-Title Keyword (Analytics, Business Analyst, and Data Scientist) (Cont.)

	Analytics	Business Analyst	Data Scientist
Managerial skills	36.96	36.63	14.98
Modeling and analysis	42.21	8.88	77.15
Communication and interpersonal skills	68.70	61.77	50.50
Programming	20.51	4.51	54.43
Scripting	15.92	2.61	62.84
System analysis and design	9.95	15.82	9.14
Tools	31.53	19.76	40.94
Web analytics	9.42	0.57	1.47
Count of job ads	147,525	365,183	46,368

Data source: Burning Glass Technologies (2018).

The concept of "mapping" skills (e.g., communications) into particular courses (e.g., the applied project course) are common to all universities. These "curriculum maps" are helpful for faculty and administration to ensure limited overlap between programs, but also to aid accrediting bodies like the Association to Advance Collegiate Schools of Business (AACSB) in their evaluation of programs.

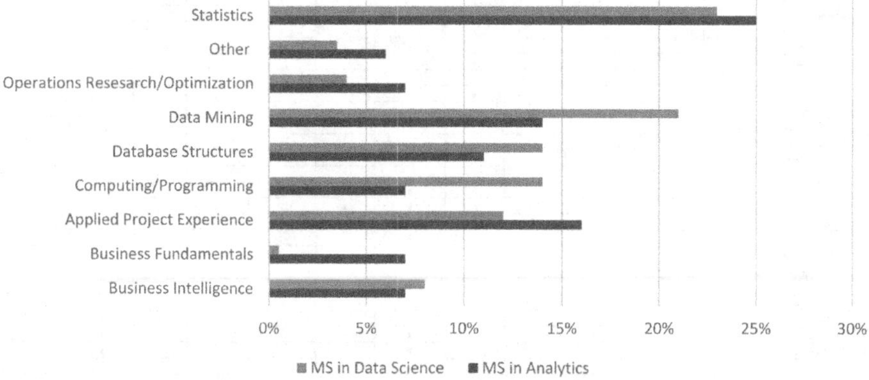

Figure 4.5   Average distribution of credit hours for master's-level data science and analytics programs by topic.

Illustrations have been created especially for this book by Charles Larson.

We have presented the curriculum map for the Health Data Science degree program at the University of New Hampshire. See Figure 4.6. In this curriculum map, the columns are the courses and the rows are the skills and competencies. Note that the map starts with more quantitative skills and moves toward interpretive skills, followed by application skills, and finally to communication skills. Thus, by looking at the first four columns and then letting your eyes blur to the right (blurring is

		Foundations	Semester 1 (e-term 1/2)				Semester 2 (e-term 3/4)				Semester 3 (e-term 4/5)	
		Pre-Program Skills	HDS 800: Health Statistics	HDS 801: US Health Systems	HDS 802: Programming	HDS 803: Translation & Visualization	HDS 900: Health Data Sysetms	HDS 903: Applied Machine Learning	HDS 905: Unstructured Health Data	HDS 901: Outcomes Research	HDS 910: Current Topics	HDS 911: Health Data Science in Practice Pt I
Mathematics & Statistics												
	Probability	X	X					X		X		
	Inference	X	X					X		X		
	Imputation		X		X	X		X				
	Experiments		X					X		X		
	Modelling		X					X				
	Time Series		X					X				
	Forecasting		X					X				
Programming Environs												
	Python				X		X	X	X			
	R				X	X	X	X	X			
	SAS				X							
	JMP	X	X		X							
	SQL	X			X					X		
Machine Learning												
	Text Mining								X			
	Neural Netwoks							X				
	Deep Learning											
Computation												
	Databases				X	X	X			X		
	Streaming data					X	X	X				
Visualization Tools												
	Storytelling					X				X	X	X
	Tableau / Power BI					X				X	X	
	R / Python applications					X				X		
	GIS / QGIS					X				X		
	Design Thinking					X					X	X
Research Methods										X	X	X
Health Care Systems				X		X					X	X
Ethics & Goveranace				X		X				X	X	X
Professional Skills						X						X

Figure 4.6 Curriculum map for MS in health data science program at the University of New Hampshire.

easy to do sometimes when looking at these maps), but excluding the electives, you can see that skills taught tend to cluster from upper right to lower left as courses progress. The curriculum culminates with the practicum experience (applied project course), which is the most immersive and applied course in the sequence. In that course, students are putting their skills into practice and within the realistic confines of existing structures (both data and organizational) and simulating impact across the project metrics. The electives (not shown) are a mix of the two, typically providing a more rounded blend of skills and application. This is one example. Different programs will emphasize different courses, skills, and competencies.

> Do not be shy about asking to see a curriculum map – it is the best way to see holistically what is being taught in a data science program.

All told, the primary way that companies engage with master's-level programs – and the frequent starting point for many university engagements – is through applied graduate project courses. To illustrate how these project courses work in more detail, we present you with two case studies shared by two university analytics programs.

CASE STUDY 1   AN ENHANCED RELATIONSHIP OF MUTUAL BENEFIT

A large energy company based in the Southeast has frequently hired students from the Masters of Science in Applied Statistics and Analytics Program (MSASA) at Kennesaw State University (KSU). The hiring managers agreed that the topics and skills taught in the classroom were particularly well-aligned with the analytical needs of their team. However, the relationship was relatively informal; the energy company would sponsor student events, hackathons, and analytics project competitions, and the faculty would forward job postings to the students when positions became available. In 2015, the energy company approached the Chair of the Department of Statistics and Analytical Sciences about enhancing the partnership through a new format that would allow the analytics team to interact more frequently and engage in regular, ongoing projects with the master's students. The goal was to not only support the program in a more formalized way, but also to create a pipeline of "known" talent for the energy company to deepen the bench of their analytics team.

The analytics project course, sponsored by the energy company, was launched in Spring 2016. The first semester the course was offered six second year MSASA students enrolled. In the context of the course, students worked either individually or on a team to classify customers and the likeli-hood of purchasing energy-efficient products and services.

Over the 15-week semester, the students met regularly with the Information Technology Team and Business Managers to clarify questions, verify results, and provide project updates. Meetings occurred approximately every other week online and in person. At the end of the semester, the students were invited to travel to the company's headquarters – wearing their best suits – to present their final models and recommendations to the senior leadership team.

From that class, one student was offered an internship which evolved into a full-time position.

Almost every semester since, the project course has resulted in at least one student receiving an offer for a graduate internship or full-time position.

Through the analytics project course, the MSASA students had the opportunity to work on a wide range of business problems. Course prob-lem topics have included:

1. Predicting potential customers for key products and services (different products and services in different semesters)
2. Estimation of a predicted power outage duration
3. Product bundling analysis
4. Market sizing
5. Solar plant production
6. Wind energy impacts
7. Event (outage, de-rates, curtailments) validation
8. Gas usage pattern recognition and abnormality detection

In the context of the project course, students have used a combination of modeling approaches including logistic regression, generalized linear models, time series analysis, recommendation system, association analysis, market basket analysis, principal components analysis, k-means clustering, and exploratory data analysis (EDA). Student evaluations of the course have reflected five consistent themes of learning:

- The project course helps students to develop confidence with trans-lating a business problem into a quantifiable analytics problem with measurable outcomes.

Students realize that effective communication is foundational to the success of an analytical project. Students reported learn-ing that what "clients" *actually* need may not necessarily be consistent with what they *say* they need.

- The ability to communicate very technical results to a non-technical audience is a necessary skill for someone who is highly computational.
- Learning to work effectively in teams is critical. While the students in the course were all enrolled in the MSASA program, their undergraduate majors included computational disciplines like computer science and mathematics, but also non-computational disciplines like psychology and sociology. Students expressed appreciation for learning how to work in teams with diversity of thought, approach, skills, and problem-solving approaches.
- Students developed an appreciation for flexibility and tolerance for changes in scope. More than once, teams received a last-minute file two weeks before the final presentation. Inevitably, the server would crash as they were trying to generate their final deliverables.

In addition to establishing a rich pipeline of "known" talent, the energy company frequently realized innovative ideas and applicable solutions from the class – although this was not their primary goal. Several of the models developed as part of class projects – such as the model developed to improve the estimation of power outage duration – have been implemented into the company's application to improve customer experience. Compared to a one-semester internship position, ongoing sponsorship of the course was a much lower cost engagement and generated more innovative solutions due to competition-orientation amongst multiple project teams. In addition, employees of the energy company have gone back and formally enrolled in the MSASA program.

CASE STUDY 2   GETTING TO THE "RIGHT" QUESTION

At Oklahoma State University (OSU), all students enrolled in the Masters of Business Analytics and Data Science program (MSBAnDS) must enroll in BAN 5560: Research and Communications. MSBAnDS is a cohort-based curriculum and as such enrolls 35–40 students every fall semester. While many enrolled students have several years of working experience, some are entering just after their undergraduate program. While the students have various backgrounds and skills, most lack project management or leadership experience. Every year, between three and six companies work with the BAnDS program to provide students an opportunity to gain this experience with real-world business data while being supervised by experienced faculty. Students are placed into interdisciplinary teams of 4–5 students at the beginning of their first semester and remain in the same company-based groups for the first academic year.

Teams are designed to ensure balance across several criteria:

1. Programming skills
2. Statistical skills
3. Industrial/domain focus
4. Project needs

The students' performance in the course is assessed across six deliverables:

Deliverable 1 – Project Proposal 10%
Deliverable 2 – Draft Report/Presentation 13%
Deliverable 3 – Project Management Process 12%
Deliverable 4 – Practice Presentations (3 practice sessions) 21%
Deliverable 5 – Final Report 21%
Deliverable 6 – Final Presentation to Client 23%

Team assessments are conducted every 1.5 to 2 months as part of the project management process; all students rate their teammates on communications, planning, team goals and shared experiences among others. Students receive anonymized comments and feedback from their teammates. These evaluations are used to conduct course correction meetings with faculty throughout the project cycle.

In 2017, one of the analytics projects was sponsored by a state licensing and regulation agency in Texas. The agency had recently undergone a data warehousing project and was interested in learning where their customers overlapped across different licensing groups. At the time of this project, faculty were outlining the outputs of the project for the students but not the business problem that it was trying to solve. For example, students were given the following information at the beginning of the fall semester:

The agency would like to have the following types of analysis run on the data. The first two are considered the critical components. The Marketing analysis would be nice to have but are of lesser importance at this time.

- *Demographics and location*
- *Compare and contrast participants in each program*
- *Churn analysis*
- *Recency, Frequency, Monetary Value (RFM) analysis*

While the students ultimately gave the company what they outlined, the project suffered from a woeful lack of creativity; the project was too prescriptive.

This was evident in presentation quality and report quality. The final projects were substantively less impressive than projects from previous years. Did the students meet the criteria? Yes, but not with the passion that the program likes to instill in future data scientists. After a debrief with the program administrators, we learned the following points that we would like to share with organizations considering similar project courses with master's programs:

1. Thinking about the end goal in mind is fine but consider starting students off with the actual problem the company is trying to solve. While these students (and faculty) eventually backward engineered the problem, it was a long and painful process to ultimately determine that what they project sponsor really wanted was to improve customer experience while improving revenue.
2. Asking the right questions as a consultant is never easy. Analysts and research-types often get stuck on the "what" or "how" and are less focused on the "why". We teach our students to think about the business problem first and all items must lead back to the business problem.
3. Please do not prescribe the outputs; let the students figure out what will work to meet the criteria. For example, when the company wanted to know "How often are the same people participating in multiple licensing areas", do not then specify that this is churn analysis. This is like giving a student the test question with the answer embedded.
4. Working with company points of contacts are just as important for faculty as it is for students. We have worked with this person on several other projects, presentations, and conferences and fostering relationships over time is important not only for analytics students but also for the program. Maintaining long-term relationships is an important investment – for faculty, students, the program, and the sponsoring organization.

A View from the Ground

A master's-level student project engagement has three main players – the faculty/program director, the sponsoring company, and the students. Here, we are sharing perspectives, including some best and worst practices.

The University[7]

One of the highest ranked master's-level programs in analytics is housed at Georgia Tech[8]. Keith Werle has been the director of the Business Analytics Center at

Georgia Tech since 2010. His Center has engaged in hundreds of master's-level corporate sponsored student projects and capstone courses. Having seen many successful engagements – and having learned from a few unsuccessful engagements – Keith shared a few reflections with the authors.

When working with analytical organization on student projects, I have found the following points to be particularly true:

1. Projects need both executive-level sponsorship **and** a project-level coordinator; without buy in and support at **both** levels, the project can too easily be orphaned, and no one ends up doing anything with the results.
2. The sponsoring organization needs to include people on the team who know the business **and** the data – not just someone from IT who gives the students access to the data. Without patient domain experts working with the students, the project can wander far from the actual business problem.
3. Be careful not to allow projects to be too tightly defined, with no room for creativity. I reject at least half the projects proposed for our students for this reason. Of the half I take, they are almost always adjusted or course-corrected before being accepted. Even then, most projects change significantly once the work has begun as the work progresses.
4. The opposite is also true – don't engage in projects that students cannot successfully complete.

> This is NOT free consulting. It is a learning objective that can also be about discovery, exploration and insights. But it has to be about the students.

5. Students need to have the freedom to self-direct – and that includes the freedom to fail. They need the freedom to try, to explore, and to fail – and then try again. I tell our corporate collaborators that if you know exactly what you want and how you want it done – then it is likely a job best suited for an employee.
6. If the project is successful, the sponsoring organization will learn something new about their data and their business – because they will see the challenges through a new set of eyes.
7. If you and your organization have never done any real business analytics projects, pricing is not a good place to start. Period.
8. Don't argue over IP. It's a deal killer. Release the death grip on non-disclosure agreement (NDA) and intellectual property (IP). Language that is too egregious will turn students off and cast your company in a light that you may not want.

The Company

Shaw Industries is one of the largest manufacturers of flooring, carpet, turf, laminate and tile. Erika Pullum is the senior portfolio manager for Supply Chain Analytics at Shaw Industries and has served as the sponsor of a master's-level analytics project with a southeastern university. Erika shared her insights on working with a group of master's students in the context of an applied analytics project course.

At Shaw, we found that university collaborations in which students and faculty work on a company's real-world business problems together can be incredibly fruitful. With appropriate preparation and thoughtful engagement, they deliver excellent educational experiences for students and significant business value for the sponsoring company. From our perspective, a university collaboration has four parts:

1. Choosing the "right" project. Choosing the correct project or problem for your university collaboration is the foundation of a good partnership. The ideal problem is neither business-critical nor unimportant. It must have high potential value or strategic importance if solved but not be mission-critical. A good way to surface these opportunities is to ideate with a team of data experts and business leaders. In which areas of your company or division can a bold new approach make a significant impact?

   Potential questions to ask are:
   - What do we wish we knew about?
   - If only we could prove X, we would ...
   - What strategic decisions are we making with gut feel instead of data?

   Once your pool of candidate projects has been prepared, you need to choose one or more to take forward. For the most promising ideas, begin to assess the available data, resources to support the collaboration project, and willingness or interest of leaders to take action.

   First, assess the extent to which data are available that relate to the project. What data exists? How well is it understood? How well does the data reflect the reality of the business unit and project? Can this data be shared? Under what terms? Are there regulatory, compliance, privacy, or legal concerns that might require de-identification or other changes to the data before it can be used?

2. Choosing the "right" team. Next, identify the organization's team members that will support the collaboration with the university partner. A balanced team of data experts, technical experts, business stakeholders, sponsors, and a leader to organize their efforts will be required. The extent to which this team is able to communicate the problem, context, and desired outcomes will determine whether the university is able to succeed in solving the problem.

   Finally, consider the business leaders who will be responsible for taking action. If the project identifies an opportunity that requires risk to increase business value, will they be willing to take action? What options will not be on the table – no matter what the data says?

Evaluating candidate projects using the criteria above will help ensure a successful business outcome as well as a successful collaboration.

3. Choosing the "right" partner. Identifying your university partner might happen before or after you have selected potential candidate projects. Important factors to consider are the profile and reputation of the educational institution, their experience with industry–university collaboration, and the terms of collaboration available.

From the business perspective, the ideal educational institution will have prior experience working with corporate sponsors and a track record of successful projects. This experience helps the leaders on the university side advise and coach your company's team, which might not have prior experience collaborating with universities. It's important to calibrate expectations about roles and responsibilities on both sides of the strategic partnership. Additionally, the ideal partner will have a strong analytical program, whether in applied statistics, data science, or computer science.

A semester-long or years-long collaboration is an important recruiting opportunity. Consider how you will leverage the opportunity to sell your company to talent at the university.

The ideal university partner has strategic advantage for your talent and recruiting, as well as your partnership.

Finally, consider the terms of the collaboration and what your business will be able to afford or accept. Consider what the university agrees to provide as part of the partnership. How will company data be protected? Who will own the intellectual property that results? Who in your company will need to approve the agreement?

4. Collaborate with Intent. During all phases of your project, be intentional about how you engage with the university and its resources, whether students or faculty. The biggest challenge at the start of the project will be imparting the correct business context for the problem. In industry, you have default assumptions that are evident to you but will not be evident to your collaborators. It may be helpful to have someone on your company team who is newer to your company or the industry, who can bring a 'beginner's mindset' and help calibrate context information. Define success carefully for your collaborators – what does a home run look like? Are quantitative recommendations or predictions required, or is a qualitative determination sufficient? Potential deliverables could be:

- An exploratory data analysis that identifies significant factors
- A model that predicts future outcomes
- An analysis of limitations of the existing data that address the problem

Most importantly, create a "safe" environment for students to learn – and make mistakes. Celebrate their successes and provide clear, constructive, and kind feedback on their opportunities to improve.

The Student

Jordan Myerowitz completed an interdisciplinary Masters of Analytics and Data Science at the University of New Hampshire. The authors asked her a series of questions related to her experiences in the applied project course which was a requirement of her program.

Tell us about the project that you worked on

A team of four, including myself, were assigned to a large healthcare company within the New England area for one of our program practicums. The company initially wanted to predict potential provider utilization throughout the year and then attempt to load-balance their providers so that they were 85% utilized. They also wanted to see how a provider's panel affected their utilization and determine if providers were seeing patients outside of their panel on a regular basis. Finally, they wanted an operational dashboard to assist with scheduling their providers.

We went into the project with much optimism and great expectations; however, the delivery of data was extremely delayed from the initial data transfer date. Issues arose regarding Health Insurance Portability and Accountability Act (HIPAA) compliance and legal issues between both the company and university's legal teams. Eventually, we received our data (after several iterations). Due to the nature of the data and the delays, our project scope was altered. We created a new utilization metric that measured the productivity of a provider given their scheduled appointments and hours working. This helped explain providers with "lower utilizations" still feeling busy and overwhelmed with patients, as a provider was often responsible for two patients at the same time. We were able to compare this new metric with the company's existing metrics with a Tableau Dashboard that measured performance across company location, provider type, provider level, and individual providers across different quarters. Additionally, we provided a timeline of the number of appointments a provider was scheduled for historically. Ultimately, the company was pleased with our work and "found our project to be the most useful out of all the projects they have worked with in the past", particularly given the reduced timeline.

What were the most valuable aspects of the project to your graduate education?

Although it was the most frustrating aspect of the project, the delays in receiving the data and the hunt and requests for more data was the most valuable aspect of the project. Classroom work, while difficult, presented us with a nice clean preprocessed dataset for in class exercises and for homework. This project more closely mirrored real-world issues surrounding the need for data and the legal hoops you have to go through in order to get it.

Sometimes after jumping through the hoops, the data is still not quite what is expected. The world of data is messy, and you're going to get dirty playing with it.

Was there anything that you were hoping to get from the experience that you did not?

Other projects within the program were able to deploy different modeling algorithms in relation to their data. This was something that I wish we were able to do with our project but was not doable given the delays previously mentioned. Given the many factors that go into patient scheduling, it may not have been modellable with the data that was available at the time.

How much interaction did you have with the project sponsor?

Initially interaction with our project sponsor was frequent – we met in person for our first meetings and emailed after. However, our data transfer was delayed, and follow-up emails entailed alternative timelines and legalese to receive it, in addition to asking about other potential resources. After receiving the initial data transfer, we set up a virtual meeting to address our questions and concerns with the data. We received additional data shortly after. With the start of the global pandemic, interaction slowed down further as they are a healthcare company and were busy trying to understand what COVID-19 meant for them. We emailed on at least a biweekly basis to address questions with the data (including requests for additional data tables). Before the culmination of our project, we presented our findings to them to see if they fell in line with what they observed as an organization, and if there were any lingering questions or curiosities that they wished for us to address.

What did the project sponsor do particularly well? What did the project sponsor do particularly poorly?

The project sponsor provided us with a breadth of interesting data that was easy to access and connect to once we had it. They were agreeable and easy to communicate with. We also found that they provided useful feedback for us to continue the project in the appropriate direction. Conversely, our project sponsor gave us data to work with in an extremely delayed fashion, and they did not give us the necessary data to answer their questions. Whether it was a test or oversight, we had to ask for more data 2–3 times in order to address their business problem. This severely delayed the start of the project and led to a stressful finish of the project.

Can you briefly explain the dynamics of the team that you were assigned to?

Team dynamics were very good. I know our professors tried to design the teams in such a way to promote a high quality, finished product, and they succeeded with our team. We were all agreeable personalities and did not attempt to shirk work. We bonded over the delayed delivery of data from our company and other delays as well. One member of the team was older and had industry experience with analytics. He sought to not be the leader but was always the voice of wisdom and was wonderful at creating and styling presentations. Although he was not the most technical team member, he was very hard-working and did not shy away from coding. The other teammates were agreeable and hard-working as well. My older teammate and I often took turns leading the project and my other two teammates provided input as well. I do not consider myself an excellent coder, but I found myself coding a lot of the project as well as creating the Tableau dashboards. All in all, every team member was committed to finishing the project and helped in various ways, even if the task was new for him or her.

What suggestions would you give to students taking an analytics project/ capstone course?
Don't be afraid to ask questions. Do your research ahead of time to see if you can answer your own questions but be sure to double-check definitions and data dictionaries with your project company. If possible, start early and constantly iterate on your finished project. You'll run into dead ends, but that is part of the process.

> Do not be afraid to try something new. It might not work for your given project in the end, but you would have learned something new and added a new skill.
>
> Jordan Myerowitz

Be sure to incorporate everyone into the team. If it seems like someone is not doing the tasks he or she needs to do, address it immediately before it gets worse and nip it in the bud. Not doing so will only create resentment and more problems further down the road.

What suggestions would you give to corporate sponsors interested in working with universities?
Due to the sensitivity of data and who has access to it, please be sure to have the infrastructure in place for students to have access to the data they need to address your business problem. Whether that be the form of HIPAA authorizations, NDA disclosures, or prepping laptops and secured virtual environment – you'll get the most out of the students if they have ample time to work on that project.

Our Summary Checklist for Working with Master's Students

Master's programs are different from undergraduate and doctoral programs. These students are more independent, almost always focused on the job market, and only spend half (or less) the amount of time in their program (12–24 months) relative to undergraduate and doctoral students. They are less likely to be engaged in research. All master's-level programs have an integrated applied project requirement – which is the primary way that organizations engage with students at the master's-level. Organizations seeking university collaborations will frequently start at the master's-level. Our summary of the primary considerations for these collaborations include:

✓ Start with the program director. Being an analytics or data science master's-level program director is almost always a full-time position. Organizations interested in sponsoring an analytics project course should start by contacting the program director rather than a faculty member, a department chair or a dean.

✓ Master's-level analytical projects should be in the "goldilocks zone" – they have more definition than an open-ended research question but have fewer parameters than an undergraduate engagement. Students need to have the opportunity to consider a wide range of options within their portfolio of skills to get the most out of the experience.

✓ The most successful master's-level projects have a committed team from the organization who are available for questions and meet regularly with the students. Again, the "goldilocks zone" for meeting cadence is likely once or twice a month.

✓ Remember that graduate students are not consultants, they are *students* and this is a learning engagement. Insights and innovation will hopefully be a byproduct.

✓ Faculty will likely play less of a role in master's-level projects than they do undergraduate internships or doctoral research initiatives.

✓ While "data science" programs are more common at the undergraduate and doctoral levels, master's programs are commonly titled "analytics", or "business analytics". However, focus less on the title of the program and more on what they actually teach. Ask to see the curriculum map.

✓ Where sponsorship of an undergraduate capstone course may or may not come with an expectation of funding, most (but not all) master's programs will expect to have the project course funded. This funding expectation may range from about $5,000– $15,000 per semester.

✓ Use the master's-level project sponsorship to inquire about other options for collaboration including undergraduate internships, doctoral-level research labs, and continuing education options for current employees.

Endnotes

1. Reid Wilson (2017). Census: More Americans have college degrees than ever before https://thehill.com/homenews/state-watch/326995-census-more-americans-have-college-degrees-than-ever-before Accessed August 1, 2020.
2. National Center for Education Statistics https://nces.ed.gov/ Accessed July 20, 2020.
3. Burtchworks Data Science/Predictive Analytics Salary Study https://www.burtchworks.com/big-data-analyst-salary/big-data-career-tips/the-burtch-works-study/ Accessed August 2, 2020.

4. Burtchworks Data Science/Predictive Analytics Salary Study https://www.burtchworks.com/big-data-analyst-salary/big-data-career-tips/the-burtch-works-study/ Accessed August 2, 2020.
5. Institute for Advanced Analytics. https://analytics.ncsu.edu. Accessed August 6, 2020.
6. Melissa R. Bowers, Jeffrey D. Camm, Goutam Chakraborty (2018) The Evolution of Analytics and Implications for Industry and Academic Programs. INFORMS Journal on Applied Analytics 48(6):487–499. https://doi.org/10.1287/inte.2018.0955
7. As an alumna of Georgia Tech, I should clarify that the Georgia Institute of Technology is an "Institute" and not a "University". Please do not rescind my membership in the Alumni Association.
8. Georgia Institute of Technology. https://www.gatech.edu/academics/degrees/masters/analytics-ms Accessed August 8, 2020.

Chapter 5

Collaboration with Doctoral Programs

Differences Between Doctoral and Master's-Level Education

Any discussion of why or how to work with doctoral students probably needs to begin with an understanding of the differences between master's-level education and doctoral-level education.

> Simply put, in a master's program, students learn how to "do stuff", while in a doctoral program students learn how to develop "new stuff to do".

There are broadly two types of doctoral programs that you will likely encounter – the Professional Doctorate (e.g., Doctorate of Business Administration or DBA, EngD or Doctorate of Engineering) and the Doctorate of Philosophy (PhD). While universities offer other kinds of doctorates (e.g., the Educational Doctorate or EdD, Juris Doctorate or JD), these degrees are less likely to be aligned with the analytical needs of your organization[1]. In Chapter 2, Table 2.1 provides the classifications of universities and colleges in the United States. Almost all PhD programs will be offered through universities classified as "High" or "Very High" Research Activity. Doctorates are primarily offered by "High", "Very High", or "Professional Doctorate" universities (see Table 2.1). Both Professional Doctorates and the PhD

Table 5.1   Distinctions Between the DBA and the PhD Degrees

	Doctorate of Business Administration (DBA)	Doctorate of Philosophy (PhD)
Preceding Degree	Typically an MBA	Some individuals begin a PhD with only an undergraduate degree and "pick up" a master's degree "along the way". In data science, the preceding degrees are predominantly computer science, statistics, engineering, or applied mathematics.
"Typical" student	30- to 40-year-old part-time student, working professional	20- to 30-year-old full-time student
Research	Highly applied	Both theoretical and applied
Funding Source for tuition and stipend	Company where student is employed or student is self-funded.	University (through teaching), National Science Foundation, National Institutes of Health, Other external research funding
Placement after graduation	Current or other private sector company	University, Private Sector, or Public Sector

are considered research degrees, both qualify the graduate to teach at the university level, and both require a dissertation. However, there are important distinctions. For example, consider the distinctions between a DBA and a PhD presented in Table 5.1.

Most master's degrees require 1–2 years of study, while most doctoral programs require 4+ years of study. However, the difference is not just additional years of study – doctoral students must engage in independent, scholarly research that will make a meaningful contribution to their discipline.

The requirement that doctoral students, both PhDs and Professional, must engage in independent research, where master's-level students typically do not (although some do), cannot be overstated. At our university, we see student applicants as well as corporate partners who do not appreciate the difference between the doctoral requirement to engage in "research" versus the master's-level requirement to engage in "projects" – master's students are more typically "doers", while doctoral students are (should be) "independent researchers". In fact, one of the interview questions that we pose for our doctoral program is "*What do you see as the main differences between a master's-level degree and a doctoral degree?*" Students who cannot articulate a difference are not offered a second-round interview slot.

I tell many of our applicants that in many ways a doctoral student in data science has more in common with a doctoral student in sociology than with a master's-level student in data science.

The point is that there are common skills doctoral students develop[2] which most master's-level students do not (e.g., conducting a literature review, formulating a novel research question, developing a proposal, producing peer-reviewed scholarship, and – the ultimate doctoral experience – defending a dissertation). These experiences and developed skills are consistent to all doctoral programs from chemistry to theology, mathematics to business.

Between the two of us, we have almost 50 years of experience in academia (Bob is older) – where many of those decades have included connecting the classroom experience with organizations seeking analytical talent. Over that time, we have worked with hundreds of analytical hiring managers – and almost all of them ask about some combination of five critical skills. While these skills can be found at the undergraduate and master's level, they are actually foundational to completing a PhD:

1. **Ability to innovate and think creatively.** At the core of any doctoral program – professional or PhD – is the ability to identify and articulate a novel, non-trivial problem, synthesize what is already known across a wide range of outlets, and develop a theoretical and/or applied framework to address the problem that will inform how people think about the same problem differently in the future. The ability to engage in innovation, creativity, and original research is increasingly a set of skills heavily sought by managers seeking analytical talent across all sectors of the economy.

2. **Communicating orally, visually, and in writing.** We frequently tell our PhD students (actually all of our students) that it does not matter how smart they are if they cannot explain what problem they are solving, how they are solving it, or why people should care. Over the four plus years of their studies, PhD students are required to write research summaries, conference abstracts, journal manuscripts, and, of course a dissertation. Students become "fluent" in writing in multiple formats (it seems like every conference and every journal has their own stylistic preferences) as well as Power Point. As they share their research, PhD students in data science must learn how to present to both technical and non-technical audiences; they effectively have to become "analytical translators" with the ability to communicate with highly technical, computational scientists as well as with less technical, but highly influential decision makers who demand that the results are tied back to the original business problem (i.e., "so what"?). In addition, most data science PhD students will have teaching responsibilities, which is a particularly robust training ground for honing public speaking skills – many of the companies with which we regularly engage specifically ask for resumes for graduate students (master's or PhD) who have teaching experience because

they tend to be stronger communicators and are more comfortable speaking to clients and senior decision makers.

3. **Leadership**. PhD students develop varying degrees of leadership skills through their research and through their teaching. As a teacher, they develop the skills necessary to motivate younger students (typically undergraduates). Through grading and assessment, they develop skills related to evaluating performance and giving constructive feedback. In the context of their research, many doctoral students will work within a larger research lab with faculty and with other students. As they progress through their program, doctoral students are expected to assume greater responsibility in these labs to mentor and support more junior research students. They are expected to take ownership of the knowledge generation process and command authority in their research area.

4. **Project (Time) Management**. Large research initiatives like dissertations require students learn the basics of project management. In the early days of a doctoral program, four years seems like an eternity. However, students quickly realize that with teaching, research, writing, and demanding faculty, four years go by very fast. Pursuing a doctorate is an exercise in project management with students recognizing the importance of developing realistic timelines, milestones, and managing the expectations of stakeholders.

For some reason, doctoral programs seem to facilitate fertility; in our PhD program, almost every married student had a baby during their program. As a rule, this event is typically not integrated into a doctoral timeline and is not part of the expected deliverables – research or otherwise.

---

5. **Collaboration**. While some doctoral programs may expect students to work completely independently, interdisciplinary collaboration is increasingly becoming more common; most students work with multiple faculty members, other students, and research sponsors on concept development, experiments, simulations, papers, and presentations. This is particularly true in analytics and data science where students are working across multiple disciplines like computer science, mathematics, business, healthcare, and statistics to solve problems and engage in research teams. As the data science community moves away from the concept of "unicorns" – single individuals who are trained in every aspect of data science – to teams of people who specialize in the different roles across the analytical continuum, the need for collaborative skills and the ability to work productively in an interdisciplinary team is frequently flagged as a "critical" skill.

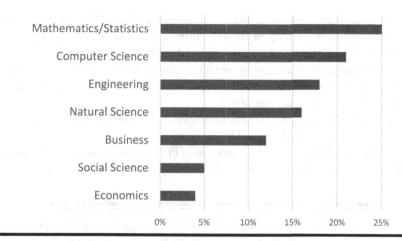

Figure 5.1   Areas of study for practicing data scientists.

In a 2018 study[3], practicing data scientists were asked what they studied in school. The results in Figure 5.1 indicate the relevance of interdisciplinarity and collaboration.

It is important to understand too that the term "data scientist" increasingly encompasses a whole category of positions that require varying degrees of specialization: data analyst, data architect, data engineer, business analyst, marking analyst, and business intelligence expert. In the context of larger analytical projects, all of these roles will be required – and required to work together.

The Rise of the PhD in Data Science

Historically, people who pursued a PhD almost exclusively sought an academic position as an assistant professor at a research university after they successfully defended their dissertation. This was succeeded by five years of research and publication ("publish or perish") as they progressed through tenure and promotion to associate professor. Academics who are not granted tenure are typically dismissed (or voluntarily leave) the university.

While some academics will stay at the associate professor level for the remainder of their career, some will pursue promotion to "full" professor, which is almost always a function of the impact their research (more about that later). Then they die. Really.

Tenured and tenure-track faculty are older than typical U.S. workers at analogous career points. According to the U.S. Bureau of Labor Statistics, the median age in the U.S. labor force is 42 years compared to the median tenure-track faculty age of 49[4] (although increasingly 49 seems very young, but we digress). In addition, just 23% of all U.S. workers are 55 or older, compared to 37% of university faculty, with 13% of faculty over the age of 65[5].

In 2018, the National Center for Education Statistics[6] reported the following distribution for faculty rank in the United States.

With the rise of data science, this progress of PhD studies to assistant professor … associate professor … full professor … followed by death … is changing.

> In our PhD program, more than half of the applicants express an interest in pursuing a position in the private sector after graduation.

According to the magazine *Science,* the year 2017 was a milestone, with an equal number of PhDs going into the private sector as entering academia[7]. See Figure 5.2. While the reasons for this shift are many and vary by field, the unprecedented challenges and opportunities which have emerged as the forms, volume, and velocity of data have evolved are contributing to the demand for well-trained data scientists who can engage in research, development and innovation in a corporate environment[8].

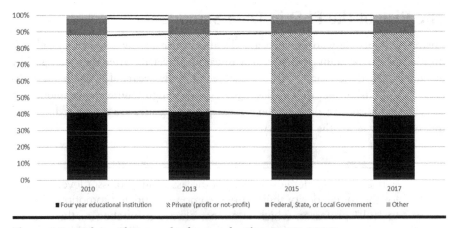

Figure 5.2 Where PhDs work after graduation (2010–2017).

Sadly, there are still some in academia who will steer their doctoral students away from the private sector and represent that any career outside of a research university is a "consolation prize". Case in point:

> At a recent national meeting of university analytics program directors, the authors listened to a professor from a large northeastern university utter the words, *"If we place PhD graduates into the private sector, we failed"*.

Yep. He said that out loud. While there was a combination of gasps and giggles, there were people in the room who nodded in agreement. Those nodding then proceeded to adjust the leather patches on their elbows and light their pipes.

Illustrations have been created especially for this book by Charles Larson.

To be fair to our nodding colleagues, the sentiment that placement outside of a research university equals "failure" for a PhD is grounded in the degree's emphasis on research. And not just any research, but "peer-reviewed" research, where the investigator submits their work to their "peers" for consideration for publication in a journal or for presentation at a national or international conference. A panel of reviewers who are recognized as experts in the area in question – the "peers" – consider the submission and provide feedback. The results of this feedback include "Reject", "Accept" (this almost never happens), or "Revise and Resubmit". Journals (and conferences) with lower rates of acceptance are, as expected, more prestigious. The level of prestige – or in academic terms "the impact factor" – of an academic's publications becomes one of the primary metrics upon which they are considered for university positions. The other metric is the amount of funding their research has received – more about that later.

Historically, only academics published peer-reviewed research. However, a study conducted by the authors in 2019[9] demonstrated that over a quarter of all publications in "academic" journals aligned with analytics and data science included researchers with no academic affiliation. Many PhD researchers in innovation labs at companies like Google, Facebook, IBM, Equifax, and Hewlett Packard are publishing their work in high impact "academic" journals in data science, thereby contributing to a more permeable research membrane between academia and particularly innovative private sector companies. So, while peer-reviewed publication continues to be the "coin of the realm" for PhDs, those coins have value outside of academia.

As an example, consider Google (of course). Google maintains a repository[10] of published research from their PhD scientists in data science, computer science, engineering, and mathematics. From Google's website:

> Our teams aspire to make discoveries that impact everyone, and core to our approach is sharing our research and tools to fuel progress in the field. Our researchers publish regularly in academic journals, release projects as open source, and apply research to Google products.

Because PhD research scientists are so important to the cutting-edge research and thought leadership at Google, in 2019, they announced that they would start conferring their own PhD degrees through Google AI research division[11]. While most organizations do not have the innovation and R&D infrastructure of Google, organizations in all sectors of the economy are increasingly seeking doctoral-level talent in analytics and data science for all of the same reasons.

Consider a second example – Amazon (of course). Amazon launched the "Amazon Research Awards" program in 2017[12]. The program offers awards of up to $80,000 to faculty members (and doctoral students) at academic institutions worldwide for research related to topics such as Artificial Intelligence, Knowledge

Management, Machine Learning, Natural Language Processing, Robotics, and Online Security and Privacy. Each funded proposal is assigned an Amazon research contact from their research division. Amazon Research Award recipients are expected to publish their research in publicly accessible peer-reviewed outlets – with the Amazon research contact. The program has also partnered with the National Science Foundation – which has historically been the primary funding source of university research – to solicit research proposals from universities to investigate "Fairness in Artificial Intelligence."[13] Another demonstration of that increasingly permeable membrane between academia and the private (and public) sectors.

In academia, the first formal PhD program in Analytics and Data Science was launched in 2015[14]. Since then, the number of programs offered through academic institutions has continued to grow to several dozen across the United States[15]. It is worth noting that these PhD programs (and these are PhD programs, rather than professional doctorates) are housed in different places across their respective universities. Common locations for data science programs include departments of computer science, statistics, engineering, or business. Some programs are housed in research units (i.e., centers or institutes). All programs, regardless of the academic housing unit have the potential to be effective collaborative research partners but may have different orientations and different priorities.

For example, programs with a stronger science orientation (e.g., computer science, statistics) will likely have a bias towards more algorithmic, process, and mathematical research. Alternatively, professional doctorate programs with a stronger application orientation (e.g., business, DBAs, engineering) will likely have a bias towards more defined problem-centered research. Programs that are housed in research units typically have a mission related to a particular goal (e.g., renewable energy, manufacturing, consumer finance).

As an example, the PhD Program in Analytics and Data Science at Kennesaw State University, is housed in the School of Data Science and Analytics. The doctoral program was structured to be completed in four years. See Figure 5.3.

As you consider doctoral programs for research collaboration, spend some time understanding what kind of research initiatives the students and faculty are currently focused on, how those initiatives are currently funded, and where the output of the research is being published.

Unlike one semester projects which are pervasive in undergraduate and master's-level programs (see Chapters 3 and 4, respectively), productive research initiatives do not readily lend themselves to transactional models that require renegotiation every time another project is proposed; university research collaboration works best under a durable, multi-year cooperative model (research lab) that enables continuity throughout all stages of research. And longer-term engagements more easily facilitate the translation of that research into new products that drive economic growth.

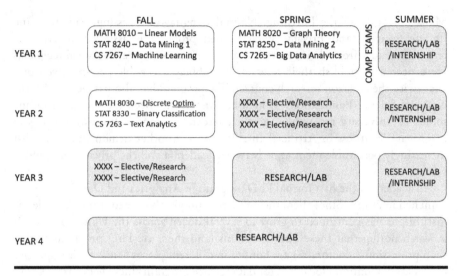

Figure 5.3 Kennesaw State University PhD program in analytics and data science curriculum (78 Credit Hours).

Establishing a Research Lab

University research "labs" are the channel through which companies can most easily engage with doctoral students and faculty.

> As a doctoral program, we look at analytical research labs as the data science equivalent of a "teaching hospital" for medical students.

These labs roughly assume one of two forms: a fee-based membership in a multi-organizational consortium or single company/single university partnerships.

The most prevalent example of large multi-organizational research consortiums that engage universities, companies and government are aligned with the National Science Foundation's Industry–University Cooperative Research Centers[16] (IUCRC) started in 1973. From the NSF website:

> IUCRC (Industry-University Cooperative Research Centers) enable industrially relevant, pre-competitive research via a multi-member, sustained partnerships among industry, academe, and government. NSF supports the development and evolution of IUCRCs, providing a financial and procedural framework for membership and operations in

addition to best practices learned over decades of fostering public/private partnerships that provide significant value to the nation, industry and university faculty and students.

As an aside, university faculty love to brag about their NSF funding. If you ever meet a professor in a bar, ask them about their NSF grants. They will buy the drinks.

One example of a recent IUCRC-funded analytics research center is the Center for Accelerated Real Time Analytics (CARTA)[17], which includes Rutgers University, University of Maryland Baltimore County, and North Carolina State University. From the CARTA website:

> The use of Data Analytics has become the "cover charge" for private and public organizations that want to provide high levels of service to their clients and customers. However, data is no longer limited to static repositories that can be analyzed at will, but now includes live, moving data sources such as video, voice, social networking, and the Internet of Things (IoT) that must be integrated across multiple sources to provide immediate, real-time decision support. Extracting value from massive and moving data hinges on balancing fundamental research, technological know-how, and commercial market intelligence.

To meet these needs, CARTA research intends to

- develop cutting-edge tools, approaches, and expertise that will significantly lower the barriers of entry into advanced, real-time analytics;
- connect members to advanced technologies and tools for easier, more efficient, and more meaningful data fusion and analytics;
- provide our members with access to multidisciplinary analytics expertise;
- build project-specific teams to optimize talent resources fast turnaround environment; and
- offer member organizations first access to our advanced analytics talent stream.

To participate in these types of IUCRC consortiums, companies pay a membership fee between $150,000 and $250,000 per year. These funds are then used to offset or "buy out" faculty salaries and support student research stipends. Research centers like this typically have a university director, affiliated faculty and multiple graduate students. The findings, publications, patents, and other research products are typically "co-owned" by the membership of the consortium.

One example of an individual organization/single university partnership is Kroger's Innovation Lab at the University of Cincinnati[18]. The Innovation Lab creates mutual benefit for both the University as well as for Kroger.

Chris Hjelm, who was the EVP and CIO for Kroger at the time the Lab was created said,

> *Kroger's new partnership with the University of Cincinnati is one more way we are investing to create the now and future of retail ... This innovative collaboration ... provides the Kroger Technology team another creative space to partner and develop solutions to redefine the grocery customer experience ... (the Lab) is a coworking community where we will build and discover the next generation of technology and talent ... Our vision is to create a talent pipeline that supports our business and positions the region as a place for digital and technology students and professionals.*

University of Cincinnati President Neville Pinto added,

> *Working with a hometown company and one of the world's largest retailers gives our university an opportunity to make an impact not only locally but also globally. This is the kind of partnership that allows our students and faculty to work on real-world challenges in a cross-disciplinary way, while offering our corporate partners added value with access to talent, expertise, research, creativity, and specialized equipment and technology.*

Given that Kroger is headquartered in Cincinnati (in close proximity to the University), this is a great example of local collaboration which will also benefit the community,

---

Our mantra for any local business community is "Eat Local, Shop Local, Hire Local".

While the details of the agreement were not disclosed, Kroger likely provided University of Cincinnati with a fixed research grant and will likely co-own the intellectual property generated through the lab. Students who work in the lab are also likely the "top candidates" for positions at Kroger headquarters after graduation.

While the specifics of university/corporate partner research labs vary, the primary topics that need to be addressed very early in the process include:

- Who owns the rights to any intellectual property (including patents) developed in the lab?
- Who owns the rights to "publish" against the findings (and definitions related to "publication" need to be agreed upon)? As a rule, we do not engage in any research labs that would preclude our doctoral students from having the ability to publish their work.
- How is the funding allocated/restricted? Is it tightly specified? Or does the university have discretion over how the funds are allocated?

Here is an example of the verbiage from one university's intellectual property clause when establishing a research lab:

> *Ownership of any intellectual property, including but not limited to confidential information, patents, copyrights, design rights, rights to computer software, and any other intellectual property rights, developed or created prior to this Agreement shall remain with the owner. Any intellectual property developed or created by Sponsor and the UNIVERSITY faculty and students whose participation was arranged by UNIVERSITY, shall be owned jointly by UNIVERSITY and Sponsor. UNIVERSITY agrees that it will grant a royalty-free worldwide, exclusive, perpetual license to the Sponsor, with a field of use limited to xxx. Sponsor agrees to bear the cost of filing for patent protection for said intellectual property. For uses outside of the xxx industry, UNIVERSITY and Sponsor are free to license the intellectual property to others, but any income received for said licensing, or from any other use of the intellectual property, shall be shared with the other joint owner on a 50–50 basis.*

Because patentable concepts that can be monetized almost always represent an expected outcome from these types of engagements, here is an example of verbiage related to patents:

> *UNIVERSITY and Sponsor shall promptly provide in confidence a complete written disclosure to each other of any Invention first conceived or discovered in the performance of the work funded under this Agreement. If requested by Sponsor in writing within thirty (30) days of the complete written disclosure, UNIVERSITY shall, at Sponsor's request and expense, pursue and obtain patent protection for a UNIVERSITY Invention in consultation with Sponsor. If Sponsor requests that UNIVERSITY pursue protection on any such Invention, and so long as Sponsor continues to pay patent costs for such Invention, Sponsor shall have a one hundred eighty (180) day period from the date that UNIVERSITY files for patent protection for the UNIVERSITY Invention or from the filing date of a Joint Invention, to negotiate the terms of a license agreement and UNIVERSITY and Sponsor agree to negotiate these license terms in good faith. During this period, UNIVERSITY will not offer a commercial license to any other party. In the event Sponsor does not request that UNIVERSITY pursue patent protection within the thirty (30) day period after the complete written disclosure of the Invention, UNIVERSITY may file at its own expense and Sponsor shall have no further rights to that patent application or that Invention.*

Returning to the topic of publication, a university may be willing to assign the monetary rights of the intellectual property over to the company collaborator/

sponsor, but they will likely want to ensure that the faculty and doctoral students will retain the ability to publish against the work in perpetuity – without divulging confidential or compromising information. Again, the ability to have innovative research published in a peer-reviewed outlet is a high priority and a primary incentive for both faculty and for doctoral students. In the example verbiage below, the University will share the proposed publication in advance with the research sponsor, NOT for the purposes of influencing the results in any way, but rather to give the sponsor the opportunity to ensure that no confidential information is included:

> *It is important to UNIVERSITY and its faculty and students that the right to publish and present information about research activities be unfettered. Subject to the limitations below, UNIVERSITY and UNIVERSITY personnel shall be free to publish and present data, information, and other research results arising from the research. UNIVERSITY agrees to provide Sponsor, in confidence, with an advanced copy of any publication resulting from the Research not less than thirty (30) calendar days prior to the submission to a journal or any other public disclosure in order to give Sponsor an opportunity to request removal of any of its proprietary or confidential information. If requested by Sponsor, UNIVERSITY agrees to remove any Confidential Information of the Sponsor from the publication or presentation. If Sponsor has not responded within fifteen (15) calendar days, UNIVERSITY shall send a second notice to Sponsor about its need to review the submission. If Sponsor has not responded within fifteen (15) calendar days of this notice, UNIVERSITY and UNIVERSITY may move forward with publication or other public disclosure. At the request of the Sponsor within this thirty-day period referenced above, UNIVERSITY agrees to delay the publication for a period of up to sixty (60) days from the date the publication or presentation was originally provided to the Sponsor so that any relevant patent applications may be filed.*

The topic of funding will obviously also need to be discussed. From a university perspective, there are typically a list of "non-negotiable" costs that they will have to cover:

■ Offset of faculty salary. In effect, the research grant will be used to "buy out" faculty time to spend on the research.
■ Graduate student research stipends. Graduate students are almost always funded through research activity. They need a great deal of care and feeding.
■ Overhead or "Indirects". Universities will apply a percentage to the top number of a research grant that will be allocated to the budgets of the office of research and to college deans to be used to support the research infrastructure of the university (very little goes to fund exotic vacations).

A View from the Ground

The Equifax Data Science Research Lab at Kennesaw State University was established in 2016 and engages faculty, doctoral students, and master's-level students. Equifax established the lab (one of several university lab relationships) for the dual purpose of developing innovative research to eventually "productize" output for the benefit of their customers and to develop an ongoing pipeline of analytical talent (primarily at the master's level).

Christopher Yasko, Equifax Vice President, Innovation Office

Equifax's Data and Analytics Center of Excellence has an established academic partnership with various leading colleges and universities to advance analytics, explore data science, and experiment with big data. We work with faculty and students in various configurations to expand our core research, explore innovative topics, and contribute to the greater good, including:

Faculty Research – collaborate directly with professors and staff researchers to complete mutually beneficial core projects;
PhD Candidate Internships – deep multi-year engagements supporting part-time employment to identify PhD dissertation level challenges that can be solved with Equifax unique assets.

The Equifax Data Science Lab has actively supported multiple academic institutions around our home state of Georgia, plus institutions in New York, California, Michigan, Massachusetts, and Missouri. I have been leading the Equifax Data Science Lab for the past four years having started and significantly grown our academic research ecosystem for big data and analytics. I've learned a few things that worked exceptionally well, and a few things that have been teachable moments.

Our multiyear academic partnership with Kennesaw State University (KSU) has been productive and continues to grow in scope and impact. We sponsor the university with an annual stipend that covers most of the cost for two PhD students, one master's student, and a part-time faculty advisor. The students become part-time employees of Equifax, requiring the same background screening and strict on boarding requirements of any lab employees. The program started four years ago, but without a clear roadmap on the specific research topics my company was seeking assistance. After developing a multi-year research roadmap, it provided both Equifax and the university a clearer set of expectations on required skills, prerequisite courses, and faculty advisor background to be successful long term. My lab also has alumni from KSU, who eagerly contribute time and energy to assisting KSU student projects. Successful PhD alumni enjoy giving back to their alma mater, enjoy physically being on campus once again, and enjoy the distraction from their daily desk stress. I highly recommend a multi-year research roadmap pairing alumni with university researchers.

One tangible benefit with a state college partnership is the mutually favorable terms in our research contract for sharing intellectual property. I've learned that universities will typically require three separate contracts of intellectual property: institutional policy, faculty assignment, and student assignment. All three can be drastically different. KSU has allowed Equifax to jointly own intellectual property, acknowledging the industry collaboration time required to be jointly innovative, and I realize the need for inventor recognition and the institutional rights. We are actively filing several patent applications with KSU, leveraging the Equifax legal department resources, plus external patent council, and we name KSU faculty and students as the inventors. KSU has the opportunity to pursue each patent and share the application costs or opt out. I've learned that each university is unique and understanding the details of intellectual property assignment policy is a critical engagement criterion.

I treat our academic partnerships holistically as an investment portfolio for my company. The portfolio shares the investment across multiple universities, with a purposeful combination of PhD and MS-level project research, and appropriate expectations for scope versus engagement duration. As a leader of an industry data and analytics research lab, I focus on tangible and *measurable* university deliverables including patent applications, industry publications that name our company, and placement of students upon graduation.

A summary of the key points that has contributed to the ongoing success of the Equifax Data Science Research Lab successful includes:

- Clearly articulated objectives, deliverables, and timelines.
- Regular meetings to review progress and discuss obstacles. In this context "regular" means 1–2 times per month. We have seen other research labs fail because of a forced "Agile" process with 2–3 "check-ins" per week.
- A collaborative approach to Intellectual Property rights, including a clear understanding of what each party needs from the research products.
- An ongoing pipeline of master's-level candidates to be considered for full-time positions.

A Second View from the Ground

We asked one of our doctoral students in analytics and data science about their experiences working in a research lab sponsored by a healthcare company.

My formative project was the pattern mining of healthcare claims data. The data was the most abstract and complex dataset I had ever seen; the medical billing code system data may as well have been another language, and the data structures were unlike anything I had previously encountered. With the help of subject matter experts at the sponsoring company, I grew to appreciate the challenge and understand the necessity of the "way they do things". The project eventually became the foundation of my dissertation research.

I do not feel I could have conceived the idea from a literature review alone. The business question posed would not have emerged from just being exposed to theory and I would have likely not have known to pursue that line of research had I not been exposed to the business problem.

The biggest challenge for me was getting all of my work legally cleared by the company to publish. Many data science journals require the data set to be available to the scientific community for reproducibility (which is a good thing), and that is a non-starter for a healthcare company. As a result, one of the limitations for me was that I did not produce the number of published manuscript(s) that I think I could have.

Overall, my advice for companies looking to engage data science doctoral students is three-fold:

First, select those projects that are academically interesting but that the company never seems to justify. Allow the projects to be open-ended, expect 66%–75% of them to perhaps be shelved or abandoned in favor of the projects that take off (the sponsor should have several projects). Reassess the projects that seem to be stalling to determine why those projects are stalling. Perhaps the project is no longer seen as useful by the assigned corporate team due to outside factors. It is very hard for a student to continue a project that they sense the sponsor has lost interest in due to no fault of their own.

Second, understand that the business questions asked may not result in the findings the sponsor wants, and that's okay. For example, I found that the short-term cost of a program actually increased initially but decreased over the long-term. This was obviously not what the company wanted to demonstrate, but the company could still use that information to improve or understand the phenomena better. These scenarios may result in the non-publication of studies, which are both unfortunate for the student as well as a negative aspect to the contribution of corporate sponsored research to literature (less-than-ideal results or null findings can still be of interest to peer review publications).

Finally, treat the doctoral student like student-consultants, as opposed to just a consultant or just a student. Plan to invest a lot of time in them upfront, and then taper that amount as the student earns their independence.

Our Summary Checklist for Research Partnerships with University Doctoral Programs

Working with doctoral students can facilitate innovation and research. However, analytics managers need to appreciate that doctoral students are not master's students or undergraduate students; they have longer program horizons, different objectives, and importantly have much deeper skills. Doctoral students are less likely to work on "one off" or "capstone" projects (unless it generates a publication), but rather in the context of research labs – either as part of a multi-party consortium or as a single sponsor/single university engagement. Engaging doctoral students will require deeper investments of time and funding than will engagements at the undergraduate or graduate levels but can generate valuable and highly tangible returns such as patentable research, published findings, intellectual property, and other forms of innovation.

Our suggested checklist for working with data science doctoral students:

✓ Recognize that research relationships with universities are typically long-term engagements that require a significant investment of both time and funding.

✓ The best way to get started is to approach the program director, the center/institute director or the office of research. This information should be available on the website. Research faculty may not immediately return your call.

✓ Doctoral students will commonly have their own "page" on the university website. See what kind of research they are engaged in and how/if that research is funded. Doctoral students are always assigned to a faculty advisor and their research agenda is almost always an extension of the faculty member's research agenda.

✓ Be cognizant of the fact that doctoral programs are typically 4–5 years long and will enroll less than 50 students. These programs should not be considered as broad pipelines of talent like an undergraduate or master's-level data science program. Given that an increasing number of graduates from PhD programs are entering the private sector, consider doctoral-level partnerships as long-term research engagements, which may generate a small number (but potentially transformational) of full-time hires.

✓ Research publication is the "coin of the realm" for doctoral students (and faculty). Collaboration with PhD students must have a research agenda. Agreement on what can and cannot be published needs to be clearly documented and agreed upon very early in the discussion process. Note that the legal department of your company will almost assuredly start that conversation with "no". But there is almost always an opportunity for mutually beneficial outcomes related to publication of findings.

Endnotes

1. Find a PhD – Types of PhDs. https://www.findaphd.com/advice/phd-types/ Accessed July 2, 2020.
2. The 7 Essential Transferable Skills All PhDs Have. https://academicpositions.com/career-advice/the-7-essential-transferable-skills-all-phds-have Accessed July 2, 2020.

3. Linda Burtch (2018). The Burtchworks Data Science and Predictive Analytics Salary Report. https://www.burtchworks.com/big-data-analyst-salary/ Accessed May 24, 2020.

4. United States Bureau of Labor Statistics (2018). https://www.bls.gov/cps/cpsaat18b.htm

5. Jasper McChesney and Jacqueline Bichsel (2020). The Aging of Tenure-Track Faculty in Higher Education: Implications for Succession and Diversity (Research Report). https://www.cupahr.org/surveys/research-briefs/ Accessed June 9, 2020.

6. National Center for Education Statistics (2018). https://nces.ed.gov/programs/digest/d18/tables/dt18_315.20.asp Accessed June 22, 2020.

7. Katie Langin (2019). In a first, U.S. private sector employs nearly as many Ph.D.s as schools do. https://www.sciencemag.org/careers/2019/03/first-us-private-sector-employs-nearly-many-phds-schools-do# Accessed May 18, 2020.

8. National Science Foundation (2017). https://ncsesdata.nsf.gov/doctoratework/2017/ Accessed May 27, 2020.

9. Jennifer Lewis Priestley, and Robert J. McGrath. "The Evolution of Data Science: A New Mode of Knowledge Production". IJKM 15.2 (2019): 97–109. Web 4 Aug. 2020. doi: 10.4018/IJKM.2019040106.

10. Google Research. https://research.google/ Accessed July 3, 2020.

11. Google AI Research Division to Issue PhD Degrees (2019). https://medium.com/halting-problem/google-ai-research-division-to-issue-phd-degrees-8a6954293047 Accessed June 8, 2020.

12. Amazon Research Awards. https://ara.amazon-ml.com/about/index.html#faculty Accessed May 18, 2020.

13. National Science Foundation. https://www.nsf.gov/funding/pgm_summ.jsp?pims_id=505651 Accessed July 1, 2020.

14. Kennesaw State University. https://datascience.kennesaw.edu/phd/index.php Accessed May 1, 2020.

15. Discover Data Science. https://www.discoverdatascience.org/programs/data-science-phd/ Accessed May 18, 2020.

16. National Science Foundation. https://www.nsf.gov/eng/iip/iucrc/about.jsp Accessed July 14, 2020.

17. National Science Foundation. http://www.iucrc.org/center/center-accelerated-real-time-analytics Accessed July 14, 2020.

18. University of Cincinnati. https://www.uc.edu/news/articles/2019/12/n20878614.html Accessed June 3, 2020.

Chapter 6

Continuing Education, Training, and Professional Development

Continuing Education 101

The terms "Certificate", "Industry Certification", "Digital Badge", and "Credential" are frequently used interchangeably. While there are some commonalities, there are some not-so-subtle differences that managers of analytical organizations should understand before sending their team off for training – either physically or virtually. The most significant commonality is that these continuing education offerings are part of a large and very profitable sector of the economy. According to the 2019 Training Industry annual report[1], total U.S. company expenditures on training and education was $83 billion – which was a 5.3% *decrease* from 2018. On average, companies spent $1,286 per "in-house learner" (employees enrolled in company-provided training and education). These figures *do not* include tuition reimbursement for degrees pursued at universities. U.S. companies have offered university tuition reimbursement to their employees as a benefit for decades – up to the annual tax-deductible limit ($5,250 in 2020). However, tuition reimbursement is typically only applied to "for credit" courses that can be used towards a degree. And educational products like certificates may or may not be "for credit". And are different from certifications. Which are different from badges. And may or may not be offered by universities. We know. It's complicated.

In 1989, Stephen Covey published *The 7 Habits of Highly Successful People – Powerful Lessons in Personal Change*[2]. The seventh "habit" is "Sharpen the Saw – Seek Continuous Improvement and Renewal Professionally and Personally". This habit is regularly cited as the rationale for an entire industry around continuing education and the (justified) mantra that individuals should regularly update their skills and become "lifelong learners". The New York Times[3] referenced the concept of "The 60-Year Curriculum", as an alternative way to think about learning; rather than consider higher education as four years of classroom learning, people should consider stretching their education over the six decades they are expected to work over their lifetime (*this would certainly change college football*).

The approach of continuous and lifelong course enrollment contributes to ensuring relevant skills and exposure to "the latest thinking" in a particular industry (e.g., how our ability to capture and analyze new forms of data is impacting consumer lending decisions or how sensor-based data is improving customer service in big box retailers). It also facilitates more seamless career changes. In a survey completed by Northeastern University, 64% of employers agreed that the need for continuous lifelong learning will demand higher levels of education and more credentials – and a majority (61%) of hiring leaders view credentials earned online as equal to or better than those completed in person (although not equal to a university degree).

One example of a company collaborating with a university to encourage and facilitate lifelong learning is the rideshare platform Uber.

Uber allows drivers who have completed more than 3,000 rides and have high customer ratings to take free classes through Arizona State University's (ASU's) online programs.

They ask drivers to fill out financial aid forms and apply for federal grants, and ASU will provide scholarships. Uber covers the remaining costs. Drivers – who are considered contractors rather than employees – are responsible for taxes on the benefit. The program extends to drivers' family members, such as spouses and siblings. Starbucks has had a similar partnership with ASU since 2014, through which about 2,000 employees have received degrees.

Analytics and Data Science – Revisited

As discussed in the previous chapters, analytics and data science are fairly nascent academic disciplines; chances are if you graduated from college before about 2015, you had very little formal exposure to the concepts, much less the programming languages, which facilitate the translation of data into information. As we discussed in Chapter 1, the definition of what data even is has changed significantly just over the last decade. Less than a decade ago, few people would have considered text or images (unstructured data) to even be "data", much less developed the skills necessary to effectively translate it into information.

So where does all of this leave existing employees who have strong domain knowledge, highly relevant industry experience, and are valuable organizational contributors, but their skills and even their approach to thinking about data are completely outdated?

> Rather than pursue a strategy of hiring (exclusively) new data science talent, managers of analytical organizations should consider opportunities related to "upskilling" existing employees. In the words of songwriter Stephen Stills, *"If you can't be with the one you love, honey love the one you're with"*.

Illustrations have been created especially for this book by Charles Larson.

There is almost an infinite number of training options for working professionals. A search for "Analytics Training" generated over a billion hits. See Figure 6.1.

Figure 6.1   Google search on "Analytics Training".

That is a big number. These results included a majority of university options[4], but there were also results for-profit training centers, not-for-profit training outlets, industry-specific training, and outlets for professional credentialing. There was a lot of paid advertising and some options that were potentially predatory. Those billion+ results can be confusing for both individuals looking to "sharpen" their analytical saws, as well as for managers of employees looking to upskill their teams.

Below, we provide some definition and distinction to those billion+ results and explain where these options may or may not fit within a larger university collaboration.

Certificates, Certifications, Badges, "Mini" Degrees, and MOOCs

Certificates

A certificate typically provides content material to help fill a specific skills gap or competency (e.g., Python Programming). Certificates may be taught in-person but are increasingly delivered online and asynchronously (pre-recorded) – which makes them inexpensive to offer. Assessment is minimal – few people will ever "fail" a certificate. Most universities, particularly larger research universities, offer certificates in a wide range of topics through their continuing education units. Currently, analytics and data science certificates are big revenue generators for universities and are offered by most large universities across the country. Certificates (almost) never generate academic credit towards a degree program and are not generally covered by tuition reimbursement. They are not standardized – meaning that the quality and content of "certificates in analytics" will vary greatly. *Caveat Emptor.*

> In the education arena, certificates are kind of like participation trophies – you will earn the certificate if you pay the fee and complete the material.

We caution individuals who think that a certificate program (particularly one online) offered by a highly ranked university will help them transition their career. Certificates are big revenue generators for universities and almost never include material developed or delivered by the academic faculty who teach in the traditional degree programs. Certificates are accessible options for people to "sharpen the saw" and engage in lifelong learning but will likely have limited impact. In addition, they should be less expensive than other continuing education options (since they cost little to offer) and should be viewed as a less rigorous option of continuous learning.

Digital Badges/Micro-Credentials

In the 2019, Forbes article "Education Micro-Credentials 101: Why Do We Need Badges"[5], author and educator Peter Greene, explains that the concept of digital badging and micro-credentialing evolved from video games,

For most of the major games, there is an accompanying set of achievements, or badges. Every time a player achieves a particular task (e.g., kill 50 zombies without reloading, drive over every tree in the enchanted forest, smash every Lego fire hydrant, etc.) they get a small digital badge on their big page of achievements. Micro-credentials take a similar approach to education.

The concept here is that the education provider will award the participant with a small achievement for each progressive accomplishment, with "digital badges" contributing (or "stacking") to a micro-credential. Think about a digital badge as a traditional "credit hour" and a micro-credential as a traditional "minor" or concentration. Several organizations have emerged as "credentialing" bodies for badging. Examples include Acclaim and Digital Promise. There is an evolving body of universities which offer badges and micro-credits in analytics and data science – both as "for credit" (contributing to a degree) and "not for credit". One university example which offers micro-credentials in analytics is the University of Dallas[6]. From their website

> Microcredentials are cost-effective, skill-based qualifications designed to provide you with knowledge, skills and abilities that can be immediately applied in a specific area...Upon successful completion of a microcredential, students receive a verified graduate credential and a digital badge from the University of Dallas .... If you decide to pursue a master's degree, UD's microcredentials can also be used as credit toward your degree.

Unlike certificates, the material content in badges and micro-credentials offered by universities are more commonly taught by the same professors in the traditional classroom.

Massive Online Open Courses (MOOCs)

As the title suggests, these are free online courses offered by universities as well as by organizations like IBM and Microsoft in which anyone can enroll (i.e., there are limited or no admissions criteria). They may be synchronous (live) or asynchronous. Platforms like MOOC.org, edX, and Coursera provide individuals with dozens of analytics and data science courses that can be "stacked" to contribute to a micro-credential. Several universities have developed 100% online master's degrees that exclusively use MOOCs. For example, the MS in Data Science from the University of Texas at Austin[7] requires enrollees to complete 10 MOOCs – students never actually have to set foot in Austin or meet with a faculty member face-to-face. As an analytics manager considering these types of degree options for your employees, determine the extent to which the students are actually engaging with faculty. One highly ranked university with a very popular MOOC in data science, actually uses natural language processing software for student engagement – online students may believe they are talking with a teaching faculty member, when it is really an artificial intelligence chat bot.

"Mini" Degree

The "mini" master's degree is a fast-track format, concentrating what would be one or two years of content into around 40 hours of instruction. Mini degrees are typically positioned as offering more and deeper content than a micro-credential, but less rigorous content than a traditional master's degree. The material in a "mini" degree will more likely be delivered by the same faculty delivering the material in the traditional "in person" degrees.

Universities may also be willing to customize the material in their analytics and data science courses and teach at your location (or provide customized online instruction). For example, our university offers collaborative corporate partners the opportunity to have select mini degrees (and some traditional degrees) taught on-site. One cadence example is where the class of 20-ish employees meet for four hours, two days a week for 12–18 months to complete the degree.

> The primary advantage of collaborating with a university to customize the delivery of on-site degrees is that the faculty member can integrate the organization's proprietary data into the exercises and examples – the data does not leave their site and is only accessed by their employees.

In addition, the "class" can work on "real" organizational projects as part of the course material. Finally, since the courses and faculty office hours are on-site, consistent attendance is higher and students (employees) can work in study groups more conveniently. Faculty would be required to sign non-disclosure agreements to use proprietary data.

Certification

A certification is different from a certificate. Again, we know … it's complicated. The goal of a certification is to validate a participant's competency or skill through a standardized assessment – much like the Bar exam for lawyers or the CPA exam for accountants. Certifications are often managed by an accrediting body and are less likely to be offered by a university.

While there is **no official accrediting body for analytics and data science**, the Certified Analytics Professional (CAP) Certification[8] offered by the not-for-profit organization INFORMS – Institute for Operations Research and the Management Sciences – has gained recognition as certifying an individual's baseline knowledge of analytical concepts. The CAP requires a passing standardized exam covering seven topics (see Table 6.1).

Here is a sample question for the CAP exam (taken from the publicly available CAP Handbook):

A clothing company wants to use analytics to decide which customers to send a promotional catalogue in order to attain a targeted response rate.

*Which of the following techniques would be the **MOST** appropriate to use for making this decision?*

a. *Integer programming*
b. *Logistic regression*
c. *Analysis of variance*
d. *Linear regression*

The answer is "b", logistic regression. This is true because the objective is a predictive model with a binary response variable (the targeted customer will either respond or not respond).

There are two important points about the CAP certification for analytics managers considering this option for their employees. The first point is that *preparation* for the certification is not standardized; individuals can be self-taught through the materials provided on the CAP website or they can take some form of a preparation course.

Table 6.1 Certified Analytics Professional Certification Exam Topics

Topic	Approximate Percent of Material Covered (%)
Business Problem Framing	(12–18)
Analytics Problem Framing	(14–20)
Data	(18–26)
Methodology Approach	(12–18)
Model Building	(13–19)
Model Deployment	(7–11)
Model Life cycle Management	(4–8)

Some universities will offer the CAP as the "final exam" to their mini-degree, their capstone course, or their certificate program. Organizations should consider opportunities for synergies between a university's continuing education options and the CAP for their employees.

The second is that the CAP does not integrate or assess any programming skills – only conceptual understanding. However, all major software companies have "stackable" certifications that can be paired with the CAP. The most well-established and comprehensive programming certifications are offered by the SAS Institute[9] – who also participated in the development of the CAP.

With such a wide range of options (and providers), why would an organization partner with a university for continuing education in analytics and "upskilling" of the current employees? From our experience, there are three reasons.

1. **Reputation and credibility**. Specifically, without a formal accreditation agency, there is no standardization or validation of skills in analytics and data science. A university's accreditation and reputation serve as a proxy in the marketplace. However, as highlighted in previous chapters, where a program is housed (e.g., business school versus college of computing) will influence the content and strengths of the graduates.
2. **Well-aligned curriculum**. While selecting "ad hoc" continuing education options from across multiple providers may allow individuals and organizations to "surgically" select specific courses to address very specific skills gaps, a wholistic curriculum including stackable badges, micro-credentials, and mini-degrees has an advantage over disparate courses because of the continuity of faculty instructors and the integration of relevant (and frequently customized) examples and applications across the curriculum continuum.
3. **Integration with research**. Where organizations are also engaged with a university through a data science research lab, there are synergistic opportunities to have the faculty leading the research to help "upskill" the employees to integrate/deploy research products. These research faculty can also share research and "thought leadership" in data science more broadly across the organization.

A View from the Ground

The following is a view of what universities have to offer managers of organizations that need analytical "upskilling" and how universities think about collaborating in the context of continuing education.

Tim Blumentritt, PhD, Dean, College of Continuing and Professional Education

The first mention of "in the cloud" by the Wall Street Journal was in a column on buzzwords published on February 2, 2006. The phrase was defined as "a term technology and telecom insiders use to refer to the Internet superhighway through which all traffic flows. It's the cyberspace between the connections to companies that provide content and individual homes". The first time "cloud computing" was in the WSJ was on March 28 of 2007. Feature length articles on the concept started appearing regularly in 2008. A headline in the November 5, 2008 edition proclaimed "Firms Push 'Cloud Computing.'"

Cloud computing is a ground zero example of how fast even major, widespread technologies are moving. These dates suggest that anyone who completed their degree prior to 2008 had zero exposure, much less training, in the field of cloud computing; every computer science degree bordered on obsolescence by 2009.

Enter professional education.

Professional education – meaning education for working professional outside of traditional undergraduate, master's or doctoral-level degrees – plays a particular role in our educational system. Whether part of large universities or as privately-owned firms, professional education delivers educational programs and credentials that allow participants to enter new professional fields or advance existing careers.

As the leader of a College of Professional Education, I am fully attuned to these dynamics. Market demands drive our continuing and professional program portfolios. For instance, computer science departments at universities do not teach COBAL anymore – nor should they. But there are many firms and governmental agencies that still have legacy computer systems that depend on COBAL, and they need people with those skills to replace retiring programmers. So even though the language is old, professional education units are still interested in COBOL because of market demand. That is our litmus test for offering content.

Professional education units serve both individual learners as well as companies that sponsor their employees in career- and job-focused education. Millions of people spend their time and money on career-focused education every year, and while estimates vary widely, U.S. firms invest billions of dollars in corporate learning annually. In return, individuals expect to obtain skills and credentials to get new or better jobs, and firms expect to hire smart, competent people then use training to ensure they can complete their assigned work.

Both individuals and companies allocate precious resources to professional education with an expected return on that investment; unlike traditional undergraduate and graduate programs, professional education programs are typically focused on developing targeted, focused skills.

So, the question becomes, in a world of shortened life cycles for most technology-based skill sets, what is the best way to maximize the return on investment (ROI) on Professional Education?

Let's start with for-profit providers. There are seemingly innumerable micro-credentialing options available to learners today. Companies like General Assembly and Flat Iron are fast-growing providers of technology boot camps. The Ultimate Medical Academy offers a number of programs that allow people to enter the medical field. Certsaffix Training "specializes in providing corporate computer software classes nationwide". The National Educators Association defines micro-credentials as "a digital form of certification indicating demonstrated competency/mastery in a specific skill or set of skills", and badges as an electronically displayed icon to represent the earned micro-credential". Just about any institution can grant micro-credentials or badges.

The challenge with these programs is that you often get out what others perceive you put in. Imagine meeting someone who tells you he went to INSEAD for an executive development program, a dead give-away since he's carrying a padfolio with a prominent logo. What he doesn't tell you is that he skipped most of the classes to experience the wonders of Fontainebleau. While he didn't learn anything, the INSEAD name still carries weight (and rightfully so). On the other hand, while most for-profit training firms provide reasonable educational experiences, their credibility is often difficult to establish.

So even if a learner takes real lessons and skill sets from a badge or certificate program, their value in the real word is minimized unless the grantor of that certificate is highly credible. Hirers and HR practitioners still depend on brand names for credibility.

Next, many major corporations have developed internal training capabilities. They go so far as to call them "universities", such as AT&T University and McDonald's Hamburger University. These units are often very sophisticated at developing training programs targeted at the specific skills or traits that they want their employees to have. The (lucky) employees who get invited to these programs get high-profile experiences and fantastic networking opportunities with other future leaders.

The ROI challenges with corporate universities arise from the very same characteristics that make them valuable. First, those corporate universities are really expensive. AT&T's website indicates that it spends over $200 million every year, which does not include support for online programs at "AT&T Learn". Given the expense of dedicated facilities, top-level trainers and curriculum development, this figure is not surprising. Second, the value of those programs to employees must be significantly reduced as soon as they join a different company. Last, the closed nature of these programs mean that participants do not get the chance to learn from people outside their organization.

Professional education opportunities at universities address some of the ROI challenges that face both for-profit training companies and corporate universities. First, good universities have good brand names, and universities are quite committed to ensuring the level of their professional education activities meets the same standards as their degree-granting programs, even if the admissions standards are different. As an indication, Harvard Business School grants alumni status to people who complete many of its executive programs.

An indication of the power of university brand names is that for-profit providers have long sought universities as partners. The largest of them, including Coursera, EdX, and 2U (which purchased Trilogy, a tech boot camp provider, in 2019) tout the brand names of their university partners throughout their web pages. Clearly, they recognize that their programs are more powerful if they are backed by academics.

Second, the breadth of universities allows them to provide an incredibly broad scope of programs. The expertise of a university's faculty becomes the raw materials for its professional education offerings. Third, universities have transcripting capabilities, which makes any credentials **permanent** and **transferable**. Graduates can request proof-of-completion even years later, and they can be certain that the university will still be there decades into the future.

Next, university programs can be customized; the programs offered by my unit can be delivered at our own facilities, welcoming individuals or teams from multiple firms, or on-site at a corporate client for just its employees.

Finally, these characteristics together mean that professional education at universities is stackable and customizable. To be blunt, universities hope to have a lifelong relationship with a learner, starting with a bachelor's degree, adding base-level training at the beginning of a career, facilitating deep expertise through a master's degree, and adding career-accelerators through advanced training and executive education.

Our Summary Checklist for Working with Universities for Continuing Education

Managers of analytics organizations and their employees have a wide range of online and in-person options for "analytical upskilling" – including Certificates, Digital Badges, Micro-credentials, Certifications, MOOCs, and Mini Degrees. Most large research universities will offer most of these options – with the exception of Certifications, which are typically managed by an industry-specific credentialing organization like the Bar Association. In the context of university partnerships, continuing education options are more commonly an extension of an existing relationship rather than as a starting point.

Our suggested checklist for extending your university relationship into continuing education for your existing employees includes:

✓ If you have an established relationship with a university, determine if they have a College of Continuing (or Professional) Education (they probably do). Determine what "analytical upskilling" options are available. Be clear on your objectives – do your employees actually need to pursue "degrees" or are they just looking to develop specific skills that their position requires?

✓ If you have successfully hired graduates from this university in the past, determine which courses the alumni felt were particularly relevant to their roles. See if those courses are open and available to your other employees. If not, see if they can be. Depending on the faculty member, they may be willing to come on-site and teach the material directly (for a fee).

✓ Consider the possibility of having a full program (like an MS in Data Science) delivered on-site with your data. While there will be costs involved to offset the faculty time and effort, this could be a particularly efficient upskilling option – allowing you to integrate your organization's proprietary data into the exercises and class examples. In this option, the data never leaves your organization and is only accessed by your employees (instructing faculty are under a Non-Disclosure Agreement). In addition, the "class" can work on "real" organizational projects as part of the course material.

✓ You should consider creating a "cohort" of employees to proceed through a continuing education module(s) together – the employees will have a more relevant experience and are more likely to integrate their learnings (creating a stronger ROI for the organization).

✓ If you are sponsoring a research lab, ask the faculty (and doctoral students) to regularly give informal talks (e.g., "lunch and learns"), where the objective is to develop ongoing exposure to "thought leadership" in analytics and data science.

Endnotes

1. Lorri Freifeld (2019). *Training Magazine* https://trainingmag.com/trgmag-article/2019-training-industry-report/ Accessed July 1, 2020.
2. Franklin Covey (1989). *The 7 Habits of Highly Effective People: Powerful Lessons in Personal Change*. Simon & Schuster: New York, NY.
3. Alina Tugend (2019). *60 Years of Higher Ed – Really?* New York Times. https://www.nytimes.com/2019/10/10/education/learning/60-year-curriculum-higher-education.html Accessed July 2, 2020.
4. Google search results can be restricted to. edu domains under "Settings" and then to "Advanced Search".

5. Peter Greene (2019). Education Micro-Credentials 101: Why Do We Need Badges. *Forbes.* https://www.forbes.com/sites/petergreene/2019/02/16/education-micro-credentials-101-why-do-we-need-badges/#692399152419 Accessed July 1, 2020.
6. University of Dallas https://udallas.edu/microcredentials/index.php Accessed May 22, 2020.
7. edX https://www.edx.org/masters/online-master-data-science-utaustinx Accessed July 2, 2020.
8. INFORMS – Certified Analytics Professional Credential https://www.certifiedanalytics.org/ Accessed July 1, 2020.
9. SAS Institute https://www.sas.com/en_us/home.html Accessed July 2, 2020.

Index

Printed in the United States
by Baker & Taylor Publisher Services

Printed in the United States
by Baker & Taylor Publisher Services